BASS
FISHING
IN
NEW ENGLAND

BASS
FISHING
IN
NEW ENGLAND

BOB ELLIOT

53,706

STONE WALL PRESS

ISBN 0-913276-06-5   First Printing

CONTENTS

To Bob Elliot Many thanks for The great fishing Bob (Howdy Doody) Smith

The late actor Bert Lahr and TV star Bob "Howdy Doody" Smith caught these bass at Big Lake, Washington County, Maine.

ACKNOWLEDGMENTS

There are many accomplished bass fishermen in this country but among the truly great ones with whom I have had the privilege of fishing, photographing as they fished, and just talking about outsmarting bass are, alphabetically, such "professionals" as the late Joe Brooks, Ed Dodd, Al McClane, Bob "Howdy Doody" Smith, Ted Williams—in comparatively recent years. And, too, long ago, the great Hank Werner, who traveled across, up, and down this nation for a major tackle concern: always in search of bass, always like these referred to above, devoting endless hours helping anglers like myself to learn a few of the lessons which can come only from such dedication to a sport and, chiefly, from fishing experience.

FIRST CAST! *by Frank Woolner*

In New England, as almost everywhere in our great country, the black bass is an extremely popular game fish. There is reason to suspect that it is *most important,* just as cottontail rabbits are the favored game of the gunning multitudes. Purists may disagree, but statistics prove them wrong—and statistics are based on polls of sportsmen who rate first choices.

Granted, we New Englanders are stubborn people and, in the beginning, it is true that we relegated all game fish other than trout and salmon to a sort of limbo. We're learning better, but it has taken a lot of time. Bob Elliot herein makes a case for the Yankee black bass—and I find myself nodding agreement with each paragraph. Like him, I am fond of trout and salmon, but I also thrill to the tempestuous bronzeback. There are days (and nights) when I wouldn't swap a fighting-mad smallmouth or largemouth for any other quarry. In their way, and in their time slot, these fish are absolutely supreme.

They aren't true bass, of course. If we want to be picky, both of the magnificent battlers found in New England are members of the sunfish family. In America there are a number of subspecies, I think now narrowed down to six by earnest taxonomists. We have two nonpareils: the largemouth and the smallmouth. For an angler, each provides the stuff of which sweet dreams are made, yet the two are curiously unalike.

Our smallmouth prefers cleaner, colder waters than its look-alike. Pound for pound, the smallmouth is a harder scrapper and a more acrobatic one: at the prick of a hook it goes into the air, often rivaling the spectacular leaps of an Atlantic salmon. It is a very tough, agile and thrilling fish to catch.

Largemouth bass are heavier, just as pugnacious, and they tolerate warmer, marginal waters. They don't jump as often as the smallmouth, usually thrashing on the surface at strike and then boring into the depths. They (as well as the smallmouth) feed on all sorts of things, night and day, and they are magnificent brutes. Every black bass is a challenge.

Both species are willing to hit baits or lures twenty-four hours a day. Both are catholic in their tastes: you can catch them on streamer flies, popping bugs, plugs, spoons, rubber worms, porkrind chunks or on a host of natural baits.

No tackle is wrong! A minority of specialists prefer the long wand, with a streamer fly or popping bug. Equally advanced anglers use the time-honored bait-casting outfit. A new royalty of sportsmen work with spinning gear. Millions of traditionalists are content to catch bass on live-lined natural bait. It's all wonderful, and it's all high adventure.

To me, the bronzeback evokes many glowing memories—the scent of sweet flag and citronella back in a day when few aerosol cans of insect repellent were available. I haunted marginal ponds where great blue herons stalked the shallows and small bullfrogs perched on the buoyant leaves of lily pads. I used to categorize "day ponds" and "night ponds," each fatuously rated according to its most productive period. The bass never changed.

Nothing is quite like a late May morning when all of the world is one fresh symphony of green and gold and pungent aroma; when you can paddle a silent canoe along a shoreline bursting with spring flowers and cast to crazy-mad bronzeback guarding their scooped-out nests in sandy shallows.

Later, after the jungle foliage of midsummer cloaks a shore and there are vast beds of duckweed, pickerel weed and pads, one hunts the pockets —tossing lures into hat-sized openings. There is a need for absolute accuracy, and then high skill after the strike, in order to wrestle that mule out of heavy cover.

Finally, of course, there is night fishing during the humid crucible of high summer. Now there is heat lightning on the horizon, buzzing mosquitoes and the ever-present muskrat drawing a thin silver vee across a black mirror. One casts to a well remembered stump or snag, not seeing it truly, but directing the lure by an angler's instinct. There is a measure of mysticism in the process, a sense of aboriginal combat. One always expects a strike, yet the inevitable, crashing attack always momentarily stuns mind and muscle.

In well populated watering places there is—you can count on it—the muted loveliness of a dance band pouring out of some shorefront resident's radio, but there are no scurrying boats or water skiers or swimmers. After dark the world embraces a long-lost, poignant wilderness.

Often one suffers to attain paradise. I fondly remember an evening at Big Lake in Maine's Washington County. Several of us had spent a day deep-trolling for landlocked salmon and lake trout, but the salmonids refused our offerings. At dusk, we took a couple of small outboard powered skiffs into the rocky ground around White Island—and smallmouth bass seemed to belt everything we threw at them.

They were beautiful bronzebacks—not monsters, but handsome warriors in the three- to four-pound class. Well, admittedly, there were a lot of two pounders! A fisherman always remembers the lunkers and conveniently forgets averages. The mosquitoes were ferocious!

It is my belief that great inland fishing and bugs go together. Bob will undoubtedly agree, now that he has retired as an official tub-thumper for Maine's grand vacationland. On that evening every mosquito in New England seemed determined to feast upon us. Although it was a warm and humid night, we wore hot foul-weather parkas and we sprayed our hands and faces with repellents—carefully neglecting the printed warning, "Avoid contact with eyes."

A black bass, whether largemouth or smallmouth, attacks like a saki-soaked kamikaze. He seems to be enfuriated, charged with malevolent energy. No "nibbles" where these characters are concerned—it's a smashing strike and a quick, powerful run, an immediate jump from a smallmouth and a gargantuan, spray-throwing surface explosion by a largemouth. Regardless of gear used, your tackle (and your nerves) will be strained to breaking point.

Bob Elliot has it all down cold. I can't think of anyone better to write about the black bass in New England, or indeed anyone as well qualified to do the job. He has been out there in the opalescent dawns, at sultry mid-day, and in the long night watches. He is a master fisherman and one of the finest outdoor writers in America.

And so to Bob . . .

Introduction *by Bob Elliot*

Before I get down to brass tacks about *how, when* and *where* to *fish* for our New England black bass, I doubtless should admit I am a late-comer to angling for this species. I've only bait-fished, plug-cast, fly-fished and gone out after bass with spinning tackle for half a century! Indeed, I caught my first bass trolling a worm—come to think of it—as my father rowed a rented boat at Houghton's Pond, eight or ten miles from Boston, during a church picnic outing.

Maybe I was seven years old, at the time. So, if we include dragging a line behind a rowboat, I could say my experience began 60-odd years ago, at that. But trouting interrupted bass fishing at intervals, so I'll only brag about 50 solid years of bassing.

Anyhow, our New England bass provide action over a longer period than our highly touted salmon and trout. Not to detract from the latter— I love to fish for them—but bass are valiant, vigorous, jumping battlers, especially on light tackle. So, our concern in this volume (and on New England waters at every opportunity) is specifically:

HOW, WHEN and WHERE to FISH for both largemouth and smallmouth black bass in our six-state region.

First, I would suggest that we dwell for a few paragraphs on the brace of wonderful bronzebacks that are native to New England. Each of the subspecies has its own vociferous champions, so I am going to be very cautious—even to listing them in alphabetical order. They are: the largemouth black bass (*Micropterus salmoides*), and the smallmouth black bass (*Micropterus dolomieui*).

In form and general coloration they look alike; yet there are subtle differences. The largemouth, as its name implies, has a slightly larger mouth, the hinge of the upper jaw usually extending back behind the eye. This is a time-worn distinguishing mark and it is far from accurate. A scientist counts the scales on gill covers: there will be from nine to twelve oblique rows on the cheek of a largemouth; more than twelve, and usually fourteen to eighteen on a smallmouth. There are other checks, such as the number of scales along the lateral line, and the fact that the largemouth's two dorsal fins are so deeply notched that they seem separated.

A largemouth black bass, in New England as elsewhere, will grow much larger than its smallmouthed cousin. The heaviest specimens are taken in Georgia and Florida, yet a Yankee bronzeback may well scale eight or nine pounds, and a few have gone better than ten. These are real trophies, yet any largemouth weighing better than six pounds is a major prize.

Smallmouths are less corpulent and much slimmer of line. A five pounder is an exceptionally good catch, and those of six or better rate headlines. The angler who collects a four-pound smallmouth needn't apologize for boasting, because he has whipped a formidable hunk of fishflesh.

In view of the weight disparity, it would appear that all arguments favor largemouth bass, but appearances are deceiving. In spite of their kinship, the two bronzebacks are different animals. A largemouth is primarily a creature of lakes and ponds, often warm, marginal waters—hence its numerical superiority as one travels southward in New England. Both species may be caught anywhere in our north country, but you will catch more smallmouths in Maine, New Hampshire and Vermont, and more largemouths in Massachusetts, Rhode Island and Connecticut.

There are other differences. Largemouth bass occasionally leap clear of the water, but usually do not: they tend to shatter the surface at strike and then fight a stubborn deep-down battle. A smallmouth—excepting when hooked in very cold water—almost always comes clear in a stunning series of reckless leaps: if he lacks the ponderous weight of his largemouthed cousin, he makes up for this in swift, powerful action.

The largemouth is a broad-shouldered bull buffalo in the brush and pads. He scares the fire out of you, sends spray flying, and wraps your line around any handy weed or stump. He's a back alley brawler, not a fencer.

I choose to be neutral. Both largemouth and smallmouth bass are magnificent fighting fish, and both are very plentiful in New England. Scarcely a marginal pond, a clean lake, or stream in our stone-wall country lacks one or the other. They can be taken with a wide variety of tackle combinations at almost every season of the year, day or night, law permitting. Collectively, the black basses are always spectacular.

I lived in New Hampshire for more than a score of years and began bass fishing there. It was, perhaps, after I moved to Maine a quarter of a century ago that I truly gained appreciation of the stamina, fighting qualities and physical beauty of black bass.

For many years, my "work" for the State of Maine involved promotion of fishing, hunting and allied outdoor activities.

Once, I fished with the late Jim Hurley of the New York *Mirror* to prove that my claims (in news releases) about bass fishing were justified. That was 25 years ago.

Mahlon Slipp, then owner-manager of Down River Camps in Princeton, Washington County, was our host and highly knowledgeable guide. Then, as now, there was a special fly-fishing season, June 1 through 21, when bass might be fished for. The limit was three bass a day but we rarely kept any, except for pictures. (Or, for one of Mrs. Slipp's famous bass chowders. She was a superb cook!)

The camps were on the West Branch of the St. Croix River. Jim and I arose early, despite late hours of newspaper talk. Although we had a huge breakfast, Mahlon put a big basket lunch into the canoe. The Grand Lake canoe had a side bracket on it (most of them now are built with a narrow stern) to accommodate the motor, but Mahlon preferred the paddle and used it except when the wind blew too hard.

I noticed that Jim's bamboo rod was a 5½-ounce Hardy, nearly identical to mine. We used heavy fly lines and stout leaders. Our bucktails and streamers were on long-shank hooks, about No. 2.

Mahlon said: "Start casting any time. Bass everywhere."

Jim dropped a bushy Mickey Finn beside a pile of driki. As the fly sank, he twitched it—*BANG!*

His smallmouth looked about two pounds. It leaped and twisted, dove and broke the surface in a wild, catapult-like explosion, time and time again. The clear water dropped from its dark sides like diamond crystals and there were, momentarily, holes in the river like whirlpools from its upward drives; wakes behind its surface skittering runs which might have been made by something far larger, it seemed.

Jim shouted like a kid. "Dollar for the first bass! Wow, look at that! Hit on my first cast!"

But I was fast to another smallmouth and I shouted: "On my first cast, too! That buck goes to the one who gets his bass alongside the canoe soonest!"

It was almost a tie. Mahlon's mouth turned up slightly at the corners. He suggested: "Maybe *I* should get that dollar."

We both reached for one but he told us, "No. I was only fooling." That was a day to remember.

Only those who fished for bass a score and more years ago will credit how good it was then. Jim Hurley wrote in his column that "Maine smallmouth fishing without any doubt was the finest in the nation," and that, "I brought to net more than 100 a day, each day for a week, on the West Branch of the St. Croix."

An area back-flooded by dams, the St. Croix West Branch then was a mass of dead standing and fallen trees. Stark, gray, twisted and, in places, snarled together like a gill net after a shark struck it, the driki was an ideal cover for bass and pickerel. Near over-hanging banks and beside large rocks, more shelter was available. Spawning grounds were everywhere. Nature (and the dams) provided protection for fish that in many locations even the most skillful caster could not penetrate.

We left flies in the upright trees and in logs, and broke hook points in rocks. But we caught bass until our arms ached and just ahead—where

Mahlon guided us—were yet more and more of the fighting bronzebacks.

Since that experience with Jim, I have fished for bass in many parts of Maine. There are doubtlessly scores of waters rarely if ever visited by sportsmen. Sporting camps in the Belgrades, in the Winthrop Lakes section and, especially in Washington County still are visited by eager fly- and spin-casters in appreciable numbers. (The laws now allow use of single-pointed artificial lures June 1 through 21.) Then, the general open season occurs and continues into the fall. In some trout ponds, there now are neither length nor number limits on bass.

Is it nostalgia that takes me back more often to Washington County? In my work—if it could be called that, when I was employed by the State in travel promotion—I fished with many fine sportsmen. I "covered" a trip made by Ted Williams into Washington County, taking pictures of him fishing for bass that were sent to the wire services at the time. He used popping bugs (an artificial, surface lure) and cast unbelievable distances from a canoe bow.

Ted came there in July and local guides doubted that he would raise bass. But his extraordinarily long casts, his experienced "working" of the poppers, brought all the bass he wanted to canoe-side for releasing.

Once, too, I fished with the late Bert Lahr and Al McClane, fishing editor of *Field & Stream.* We were on Big Lake, Scraggley Lake, Junior—many others. All had bass, but it seemed to me that fishing was slower than it was a quarter of a century ago.

On that occasion, we enjoyed fishing and a cookout with Bob "Howdy Doody" Smith, who then had quit television so he could live on the shore of Big Lake and do nothing except bass fishing. (He's now back on TV, of course.)

In more recent years, I have fished with one of the finest gentlemen I have ever met—Ed Dodd, who draws *Mark Trail.* Guided by Leslie Williams, Grand Lake Stream, we have caught fish to a degree reminiscent of the good old days—at the Machias and Wabassus Lakes in that area.

We have, incidentally, found Williams to be an outdoor cook matched only by Mrs. Slipp, who prepared those bass chowders inside her camps on the West Branch of the St. Croix River.

Joe Brooks, the late fishing editor of *Outdoor Life,* was a bass fishing companion in 1971. His casts were like those made by Ted Williams, when I photographed Ted in the same general section of Washington County, Maine, years ago. Joe was a popping bug fancier, like Williams, too.

Today my old Hardy rod is a collector's item and a new one, weighing a bit over 5 oz. gives me satisfying, long casts. This 8 ft. 6 in. Palakona cane flyrod uses a No. 8 line, and has plenty of action. I like the (Hardy) Zenith Multiplier reel when fishing for bass with this rod. It stores all the line and backing ever needed for bronzebacks. (To fish for Atlantic salmon in eastern Maine, the same outfit is adequate for these fine battlers.)

The Hardy Jet Set glass rods also make good bass fishing tools. They cost somewhat less and come in several weights and lengths. For bass, Nos. 8 or 9 are good and 8 or 9 lines match them well.

Flyrodding for bass is, of course, only one of many methods. It is well to remember that the first tackle combination actually developed for this species was bait casting. The famous Meek Reel, a quadruple multiplier, came out of Kentucky, spread southward, and then into every jade green waterway of the United States where bronzebacks reigned.

There is still nothing to match the efficiency of a well built bait-casting rod with a smooth running quadruple multiplying reel, a line testing twelve to fifteen pounds, and plugs or other lures to defeat largemouth bass in the brushy, weedy pockets of marginal ponds. This rig combines tack-driving accuracy with power and control under trying conditions.

In relatively open waters, spinning tackle may be an excellent choice: it is a weapons system, light, yet able to deliver a lure or bait right on target. The new spinning reels feature silk-smooth drags and, in lake or river fishing where shoreside cover is no major obstacle, a man can go very light and enjoy superb sport.

We'd better not forget the still fisherman who enjoys live-lining a redfin shiner, a hellgrammite or a crawfish as bait for a bronzeback with blood in its eye. We all fish for fun and the tackle doesn't matter—so long as it gives the quarry a sporting chance and gives *us* memories to cherish.

We'll argue about rigs and baits and techniques, but we'll never deny that the New England black bass will test our equipment on those occasions when we get into fast action on any of the hundreds of fish-filled waters in our six-state region.

May we meet on river, pond or lake: not once, but frequently, and exchange yarns and bass fishing lore to our piscatorial hearts' content.

In the following pages, I will have my "say." This is the privilege of a writer—to speak first—by printed words.

1

BAITS AND BOTTOM FISHING

In many New England lakes and rivers, smallmouth bass move into deeper water during warm weather periods. When they are in spring-fed, cool water areas, they are more apt to lie in somewhat shallower places, of course. However, they still frequent the deep "holes" and when these spots are close to sections that support minnows, frogs, insects and similar bass foods, they swim up and out of the depth and chase what might be termed "baits" into the shallows.

Largemouth bass frequenting marginal ponds observe a somewhat different schedule: they are likely to haunt brushy, weedy and pad-bedded shallows throughout the summer, going deep only in the low temperature periods of spring, fall and winter. Both species are found on shallow spawning grounds in late May and early June.

A simple rule to remember is this: *Bass have to eat and find shelter.* Precisely as humans and other forms of life must have food and places to live nearby, so do bass. Ideally, then, water containing rocks, old stumps, weed patches and cool, deep, sheltering spots, with large trees overhanging undercut banks to provide shade and darkness, is the most acceptable to bass.

The arguments about comparative effectiveness of artificial lures and flies versus natural bass foods are age-old wherever and whenever sportsmen meet.

I prefer to use flies, first of all; then surface artificials (poppers, etc.); next, casting rod plugs and spinning lures; and finally baits—just because it seems to be more sport to outwit a bass in this order.

Still, it is difficult to defend "make-believes" as superior to baits, except when bass are on their spawning beds (smallmouths in early spring) or when night fishing is done for largemouths. Then, wild-action plugs like a black Jitterbug are effective. (But more of this in another chapter.)

Here, then, are popular bass baits in New England:

Hellgrammites (the dark-color aquatic larva of Dobson flies), crawfish (the small, lobster-like fresh-water crustacean sometimes called crayfish especially by zoologists), earthworms (particularly those worms called variously nightcrawlers, nightwalkers and nightrunners), grubs, live minnows, grasshoppers, frogs and even mice.

There are others, too. Largemouth bass will hit nearly all kinds of food in its natural state. If you should want to justify bass fishing to a bird lover, you can tell him that I have seen "bigmouths" leap out of water a short distance and seize darting swallows or small songbirds hovering on the lower stems of swale grass.

And, in a side reference to worms, I once said jokingly: "The farther

Ideal smallmouth bass water—rocky shore, cool, clear water.

north you travel and consequently the colder the climate, the faster the worms move. They are night*crawlers* in New Hampshire and southern Maine; night*walkers* in central Maine, but night*runners* up north near the Maine-Canadian boundary."

To go a bit farther afield:

It is wise to check state fishing regulations before using any kind of live bait in New England. Usually it is so-called *cold*-water species, like trout and salmon, that officials are trying to protect. Bass are found, however, in some places that also hold trout, so the laws may be more restrictive than first appear logical.

The idea is this: Many New England waters are being reclaimed and then stocked with brook, brown or rainbow trout. Rotenone or another chemical is broadcast in a pond to destroy competing fish. Then the water lies dormant for a time and finally trout are stocked.

Fisheries authorities know that any given body of water can support only a certain number of gamefish. Since trout are the preference of so many, they are given every opportunity in reclaimed ponds to become dominant. Introduction of minnows (particularly "spiny-finned" fishes) starts the competition for food and space all over again. The work of fisheries' biologists in preparing a pond for trout and stocking them then is wasted. So laws are strict on some waters. Better read your book of regulations or inquire first.

Ice fishermen oftentimes in the past dumped their minnow pails into the lakes when fishing was over for any given period. Only recently have the disastrous results of this come to light in New England. Thus, beginning fresh-water anglers in particular, but others too, may not be aware of the consequences of their unlawful use of certain baits.

In Maine, for example, *"It shall be unlawful to take, sell, use or have in possession, either dead or alive, for use as bait for fishing in the inland waters of this state, any pickerel, goldfish, yellow perch, white perch, bass, sunfish, crappie, hornpout, carp, or any spiny-finned fish."*

Smelts usually are used, where Maine waters are not restricted to fly-fishing, in trolling for landlocked salmon and trout. Bait dealers stock them in places near lakes that are open under the General Law and also usually have them available for bass fishing.

In coastal areas, bait dealers (and those who get their own baits) have mummichogs (killifish) readily accessible, for these are common in brackish water back from the sea. Thus, at least two species of acceptable minnows can be obtained for baiting bass.

Before we leave the subject of laws, nevertheless, I would point to another one which might not be widely known, especially by salt-water fishermen who have turned inland to try their luck in Maine lakes, ponds or rivers:

"Whoever deposits any meat, bones, dead fish, or parts of the same, or other food for fish in any of the inland waters of the state for the purpose of luring fish, known as 'advance baiting', shall be subject to the penalties provided in section 3060, and costs of prosecution, for each offense."

This, called "chumming," is of course often done by commercial fishermen at sea; it is therefore well to know it is prohibited on inland Maine waters.

(Most New England states have similar regulations, although fishing laws in Maine are perhaps more restrictive than is usual, nationally.)

It seems to me, looking back to so many years of fishing in our six-state region, that I began—as most sportsmen do—using baits to catch bass. Once, as a young boy, for instance, I angled at Harvey Lake in Northwood, N.H. It was then little settled in that section; though now numerous cottages are to be found there.

Another youth and I had turned over stones in a southern New Hampshire brook and had come up with a dozen hellgrammites. On the lake, we hooked No. 4 snelled hooks (the same ones we used for trout, then) under the "collar" of a hellgrammite apiece, being careful not to get nipped by the savage-looking larvae—handling them like small-scale lobsters, our fingers behind the little jaws.

With no wind or current, we did not add sinkers to our lines. We wanted the hellgrammites to crawl about on the bottom naturally.

Lowering them boatside, then, we slacked off on our soft-braided lines and drifted slowly by pulling occasionally on the oars until we were at a depth of some twelve to fifteen feet. In this spot on other occasions we had taken bass by this method.

So, we lowered our anchor carefully and tried to be nonchalant before each other.

"Probably won't catch any, anyhow," I said.

It was a cloudy day, yet without rain. We were patient. Half an hour went by. Once in a while, one of us would haul in his line, inspect the bait, and lower it to the bottom again.

Half asleep, I sensed, rather than saw, that my line was moving slowly off. "Something's taking it!" I cried.

"Easy does it," my friend urged. "Let him get it good."

The line went out several yards, then stopped. I held my breath . . . tried to wait. When I tightened the line, I found my luck was stronger than my judgment. Despite striking the bass too soon, he made a second lunge and somehow became impaled on the small barb.

He jumped, on the light rig, like so many smallmouth bass were to do for me in the many years that followed. His bronze-greenish sides glistened each time he surfaced and dove. Water cascaded from his twisting, thrashing body. My heart beat faster and in my youth I grew highly ecstatic. Yet, never in my life have I failed to experience the excitement of watching a fighting black bass try to shake the hook—to seek to return to his lair.

I could not bring myself then to release the fish unharmed. That is too much to ask of a boy, eager to prove to his family back home that he knew how to catch bass. But, after my companion had caught two other smallmouths and I had boated a mate for my own, we were satisfied to quit for the day.

"Hooked" ourselves, nevertheless, from that and other early bass fishing excursions, we stole away on every opportunity to Harvey and other lakes. Not always successful, we caught enough fish to keep our enthusiasm high.

Using crawfish for bait, we pierced them through the tails, so they could crawl naturally on the bottom. When live minnows were our choice, we ran the barb under the back fin; again, so the small fish could swim naturally.

Earthworms were hooked through the small hard ring near their heads, then the barb was run in and out a few times to keep them impaled. Never so tightly, though, that their wriggling motion was hampered.

Using nightcrawlers, we added small sinkers or split shot on the leaders above our baited hooks. Then, the lead would find and rest on bottom and the worm would float above the sinker a few inches and more. A bobber on each line indicated when it went under the surface that a fish had taken the worm. We learned to wait until the bobber stayed under a minute or two before we struck the bass.

When action was slow, we jiggled the lines and bobbers to send messages down below! Thus, the worms would wriggle enticingly and occasionally, at least, a reluctant smallmouth would hit.

A word about "picking" these night-time worms. Certainly in New Hampshire and Maine (we never happened to seek them in the other regional states) nightcrawlers are abundant. If you haven't sought them and if you are a person with a sense of humor, you'll get a kick out of this kind of bait hunting.

Smallmouth bass lunges up and out on rise.

First, a fairly rich soil is desirable. Then, in order to see the worms readily, a mowed lawn is best. Following a rainstorm, or when lawns have been watered, the night worms come up and lie on the surface of the grass. One end stays in a hole and if you aren't fast in your "picking" the worm will slither back out of sight in the fraction of a second.

You need a container with some moss or loose soil inside, and a flashlight with a red lens. If this is not readily available, red lipstick can be used to lightly coat the lens.

Finally, practice makes perfect in picking night worms, as in any other activity. It's mostly a matter of moving slowly in a crouching position across the grass, swinging the light beam steadily in kind of a "painting" fashion until that long brown worm is seen, stretched out and apparently immovable. (Nightwalkers look twice the size of common earthworms and, under the light at night, they appear even more elongated.)

Now, you get close enough, cautiously, to reach down and close thumb and forefinger quickly over the suddenly struggling worm. Before you can catch a breath, the nightwalker already has slithered part way into its hole in the grass. If you yank on it, you may break the worm in two. So, a slow, steady pull is best.

In central Maine, in the state capitol city of Augusta, the soil is clay and retains a lot of water following a rainstorm. Lawns in front of residences, well-kept grass around state buildings and greens on golf courses are perfect "territory" for picking the night worms. My two younger sons became adept at picking worms when they were of school age. They brought in pails filled with nightwalkers and we had to cry, "Cease and desist!" on several occasions.

Like other kids, they offered night worms for sale to anglers. Business didn't get too brisk. Nowadays, it is a better bet, particularly during the hot weather months, when Maine's population more than triples. A great many vacationers do fish and some of them are ready customers for nightwalkers.

Indeed, with nuclear energy plants replacing or supplementing other electric power installations, wastes are almost certain to kill sand- and blood-worms in tidal flats and nightcrawlers could, I believe, become an adequate if not equally effective, bait for striped bass and other salt-water species that now are often sought by fishermen using blood-worms. There is a close resemblance between nightwalkers and the salt-water worms, although the former are smaller, of course.

In New Hampshire, I lived in Hampton, inland from the ocean a few miles. We used to pick nightcrawlers on lawns in front of the library and

19

other public buildings and were occasionally checked by officials, who
wanted to know "What the heck is going on?" When they looked into our
containers their curiosity and concern were mollified. Some of them even
became converts!

Once, frustrated by smallmouth bass in lakes in central Maine, several
of us decided we should go find some night worms to use next day.

We were staying in a camp with a friend in the small town of North
Whitefield. He found his flashlight and away we went, driving to the lawn
fronting an estate and walking out boldly to search for nightwalkers.

Having passed a long evening talking after dinner that night, it hadn't
occurred to us that midnight had come and gone by the time we started
worming.

No lights shone in the big white house. "The judge won't mind. He's
a fisherman," our friend explained, when we voiced apprehension about
our unheralded visit.

Just then, a number of lights flooded the house windows and a sten-
torian call wanted to know "Who the hell is out there?"

"It's me" (giving his name) our friend explained. "We're picking
worms. Bass haven't been hitting anything. Thought they might take
nightwalkers."

"When you get a pailful come inside and we'll have a drink," the judge
shouted. "I'll tell you where to fish in the morning."

Confirmed anglers well know that there just isn't any similar camarade-
rie to that among sports fishermen. This is particularly true in Maine. If
you want to become a VIP of that state, always carry a fishing rod and a
shotgun in your automobile and have similar equipment on display in your
home and office. Immediately, you will be recognized as a dependable,
honest, friendly individual.

Even if you're just passing through, sportsmen will begin a conversation with you when they see you're a fisherman or a hunter.

Once, years ago, I had a similar experience while I was living in New
Hampshire. A fishing buddy remarked that we should have brought a can
or two of beer along, "if I had known we'd be here all day and half the
night," he concluded. (We were fishing a pond some 50 miles from home.)

There were several cottages on the shore.

I rowed our small boat near one and saw that, as I had suspected would
be the case, the owner and a few of his neighbors were having cocktails.

"How's the fishing?" he shouted.

"Not good," I replied. "The drinking is worse. We didn't plan to stay
so long and failed to bring any beer."

"Come aboard! Plenty of it here," he cried.

After a brief, friendly visit, I remarked: "You know on a big lake, stopping by enough cottages like this, a fellow could not only begin to feel his drinks, he could save a lot of money."

The owner laughed. He knew it was our way of saying thanks.

Down through the years of my sports afield, I have met and fished with many fine people in all walks of life. They have cared only about the sport of fishing. Unless I brought up the subject, their business or profession was not referred to. They were out and away from all responsibility. *Just fishing.*

Often people I haven't seen for years write or telephone to me. The subject is fishing or hunting. We say we've been well or ill. That over with, it's "How's the bass coming? We've got to get together again and give them a try once more."

To HOW, WHEN AND WHERE TO FISH for bass, we should add: HOW TO WIN FRIENDS AND MEET SOME OF THE FINEST PEOPLE ON EARTH.

So, back to the Maine judge's home once more. He proved to be such an interesting conversationalist and knowledgeable sportsman that we all lost a good night's sleep and had bacon and eggs at his table before leaving. He gave us explicit directions on where to use those worms from his lawn to catch outsize smallmouth bass. Our fishing was highly successful, thanks to him.

What other sport attracts people like fishing?

Explicitly, now I should add a few words about the use of attractors with baits.

I have found that small spinners above worm-baited hooks (five or six inches up from the hook shank, tied in, on the leader) add attractiveness and draw bass more often to take worms. When fishing with hellgrammites or crawfish, nevertheless, I personally prefer to let the baits fall naturally to bottom and to fish them without even a sinker, as stated earlier.

Another bottom-fishing lure (and, we are getting away from *natural* baits fished deep) is the medium-sized feather jig. This is intended as something for bass to hit, of course, not an implement with which to hook or "jig" fish by striking them in the side or another part of their body. Jigging in the latter manner is illegal in some New England states, if not in all of them, where fresh-water species are concerned, other than suckers and eels, which in certain places may be speared legally. (Suckers, in Maine, for example, may be taken in rivers, brooks and streams that are open to fishing, by use of hand spear; only during April 1 to June 30,

Bass thrashes on surface to avoid net.

however, and only by licensed sportsmen; that is, by those who have regular fishing licenses or who otherwise are entitled to fish in Maine.)

Again, I am considering artificial feather jigs, that are manufactured, sold and used for the purpose of exciting bass and other gamefish to take them as though they were a form of food—in their mouths.

Once, another writer and I were fishing for smallmouth bass in northern New England. I had used streamer flies and my companion had been casting surface lures. We desperately wanted sizable bass to photograph but all we had taken on that particular day were small and we had caught only a few of those. We remarked to our guide that we "guessed we would have to come back another day."

He picked up an ancient spinning rod apologetically, reached in his battered tackle box and drew out a weighted feather jig with black feathers. Tying it on directly to the monofilament, he dropped it over the side of the big canoe we were riding in.

As the line slackened when the jig hit bottom in perhaps twenty feet of water, he lifted the rod tip a few times and leaned back to set the hook. Soon, a fish of at least three pounds slapped in the bottom of the canoe.

In silence, as though to show us where the bass were lying that day, he changed to a similar size feather jig but this one dressed in bright yellow. It seemed as if he caught a mate to his first bass immediately. Anyhow, it didn't take long. We were so red of face we could only gasp and sputter.

I wondered if he had delayed fishing the jigs until he was over a bass hole with which he was familiar. You don't find out from a New Englander unless you ask and when fishing is concerned the answer surely will be evasive.

"Could take two bass at a time occasionally, if you tied two jigs on the same line," he wagered. "Don't know if that's legal or not," he said, looking at me, a stickler for the laws, and smiling. "Anyhow, got two for your pictures."

Besides the feather jig as an effective bottom lure for bass, I have found that spoons also are productive on occasion. If treble or double hooks are removed and a bait (worms) added to either the feather lure or a spoon, this combination also can entice reluctant bass to strike near bottom.

Porkrind strips, fished on a line with sinker-and-hook only, can occasionally take bass near bottom. It is better, in my opinion, to use the strips behind spinners, spoons or feather lures, when trying for bass down deep.

There are other combinations. A big marabou streamer fly is good. It can be red and white in color, for example, be tied on a No. 2 long shank hook and either weighted by winding strip lead around the hook before dressing it, or by sinking the fly on a wet flyline. Another choice is to fasten the fly to a small spinner and, finally, to add a couple of split shot to your leader.

The more naturally the fly is fished the better. For this reason and others (such as it's more fun to take a bass on the lightest possible un-weighted fly), I use a sinking flyline to get the pattern down where the bass should be when they are lying deep.

I have not emphasized the depth of water in which I find bass and decide that fishing off the bottom is the more likely way—on that occasion, at least—to catch them. In shallow ponds and rivers, "deep" may be six to ten feet. In larger lakes, particularly where surface waters warm up appreciably, "deep" may be 25 feet. And, it may be even more.

Some anglers decide that larger gamefish will only be at those depths which are suitable to small baitfish. (A little minnow cannot survive as far down as his predatory "heavy.") However, I believe bass, both largemouth and smallmouth, may lie in a whole lot deeper water than might be ex-pected. Like lake trout, I expect bass occasionally at least have their aquatic "homes" in 30 feet of water and more but that, again like lakers, they swim up to those levels where the minnows school. After eating their fill, the bass drop back into the deep holes, I assume. Lethargic, just as we are when our bellies are full, bass are lazy, bottom fish. I thus maintain that small-mouth or largemouth, replete, stuffed, gorged, satiated, are less prone to hit my proferring of hellgrammite, crawfish, worm, minnow or artificial lure than when I can surprise him as he is actually feeding.

What does this mean? It says that I suggest you study the waters you fish for New England black bass, trying to pinpoint those shelves edging the deeper places. A fish finder can save a lot of time. Most states have lake survey maps that show depths quite readily. As a test, you can bend on a little hook, drop it over and catch a few baitfish. Now, you will have proven that this is one logical place for bass to search out lunch. Like a voracious black shadow, he will ascend from his dark lair and literally drive through schools of baitfish, killing some, swallowing many. Be there precisely then, with a minnow-baited barb, and you will have fast action.

If you see injured and dying minnows floating on the water when nobody else is fishing nearby, you can be certain gamefish are feeding. It may be a hungry pickerel or two—but it *could* be a bass! Things like this keep us going back to those specific locations where we have had excep-tionally fine fishing on other occasions.

Remember, as I do, that commercial fishermen at sea find Georges Bank and similar shoals hold feeding fish.

Some New England rivers have rapids; bass pools lie above and below falls in quieter water.

Thus, we have worked our way off the bassy bottoms (logically, I trust) to medium depths where lurk the quarry we are seeking.

So, too, we have found our way to the end of a chapter: not forgetting bait fishing for smallmouth and largemouth bass in New England waters, but considering the use of the natural bass foods in their normal feeding depths, instead of in their murky and shadowed "homes" where they are more prone to sleep away their inertia.

2

SOME USUAL AND UNUSUAL USES OF THE SEMI-FLOATING BAITS AND ARTIFICIALS

Naturalness in offering baits and artificial lures to any gamefish is important. It can mean the difference between bass on a stringer and little or no action at all.

How do I present a bait in a natural way? It was a good friend of mine (who then lived in Rhode Island and since has moved to Connecticut) who taught me a few "tricks of the trade." We were attending a conference of outdoor writers in Vermont at the time. When the "farm boy," as he called me, couldn't seem to entice those Green Mountain bronzebacks in any of the usual ways, some of my friend's secrets were divulged.

We were trying our luck and skills on a stretch of the Missisquoi River in the northwestern section of Vermont. The river also contained rainbow and brown trout—which we were not averse to catching—chain pickerel, perch, etc. It was the smallmouth bass, nevertheless, that we were chiefly trying to catch on that occasion.

My companion removed a split shot from his worm-baited tackle and, picking up a piece of dry bark from the riverbank, he carefully set it afloat, with the hook and worm dangling just over one edge of the little bark raft.

It drifted slowly in the sluggish current at that point, as he fed out line to keep pace with its movement. Fifteen or twenty yards downstream the current eddied in toward an overhanging tree. The U-like portion of the river here was lush with water weeds.

As the bark nudged against the weeds there was a smashing rise which tossed the light "raft" into the air like so much paper. I realized this happened but the major impression was one of a beautiful smallmouth, skittering on his tail, diving, coming up and out in high, arcing, surface-shattering drives which left us both breathless. We shouted like kids.

The bass was struggling toward his hiding place under those weeds but my friend kept the pressure on and finally turned him toward the waiting net.

"It doesn't work every time, of course," I was informed, with the acceptable modesty one might anticipate under these circumstances, "but, as you have seen, it can really pay off."

"Yeah," I agreed. "So it can."

We didn't make much of a killing that day. The raft-floating brought another strike further downstream. We took a pair of pickerel, casting. And my buddy struck, played and brought to net the other smallmouth as skillfully as he had the first bass. This really saved the day for us.

When I resorted to casting a plug with a bait-casting rod, he suggested something else in the way of variety and naturalness.

Tail-walking bass is inverted U on descent.

"Can you cast the plug so it lands on that big rock near the bank?" he asked. "Then, let it stay there a minute and twitch your line, so the plug falls off into the water?"

"Well! I'd have you know I used to do some informal bait-casting in New Hampshire years ago, my friend. I was on the sportsmen's club squad, as a matter of fact."

Lucky for me and my bragging, the plug landed right in the middle of that rock, first cast. "Good," he said. "Hold it now!"

After a pause that pleased his sense of timing, I lifted my rod tip and splashed the plug into the river.

A boasting-size bass came up under the plug and the next split second he was imitating the fighting-mad lunges of the smallmouth my friend had caught from his tiny raft device. I lost the fish but I still remember the trick. It has served me well on a number of other occasions.

Now it was my turn to demonstrate a few devious ways of catching bass. We made a date to fish together the following weekend in New Hampshire. Our choice of a lake was Wentworth in Wolfeboro. Feeling lazy, we began by trolling lures that rode just under the surface—Dardevles and Mooselook Wobblers, and other similar artificials.

When nothing much happened, I began see-sawing the boat, making long loops out from the shoreline, then cutting back toward the shore. This caused the lures to drift in much closer than when we maintained a straight course.

"It's like teaching a dog to quarter a field," I said to my companion. "Maybe the bass are right in close today."

Apparently they were. About the third looping turn, as our wobblers ran in almost against the bank, we had double smashes simultaneously and shortly hung the pair of smallmouths on a stringer for pictures later on that day.

"Well, 'City Boy,' that shows you how to locate the bass. Now we can cast for them. I'll run the motor for a while. When you get arm-weary, you can play captain and I'll cast for bass. Okay?"

"Why don't you leave your line out and troll while I cast?"

"Wouldn't work too well. Lure would sink, since we have to go slow in order for you to cast effectively. I'd probably get my wobbler hung up on bottom. We'll just take turns. No sweat."

Whatever artificial he cast seemed to bring savage strikes that kept us both busy all the while. Occasionally we ran the boat offshore into deeper water but the bass just were not in evidence except close in. His wobblers, small spoons, spinners, little plugs, caught in overhanging limbs, shoreline rocks and partly submerged logs, here and there, but when anything landed within a few feet of the banking correctly, it was smallmouth suicide.

There were so many, we simply played and returned all but the first pair to the lake. For, when I took over fishing, the results were the same.

The next weekend I fished Wentworth alone and the conditions had changed dramatically. The only bass I brought boatside were those that hit in deeper water, often 25 to 50 yards offshore.

Obviously, the bass were still on their spawning beds the first visit we made together—this, despite the fact that it was late in the spring to find them spawning. And, on this score, smallmouths may be on their beds as early as late May and as long afterward as the last of June and even more rarely into the first of July in northern New England. Maine's special season with single-pointed artificial lures and flies is established to coincide with the spawning period in average years. The dates are June 1 through 21, it will be remembered.

Since smallmouths may be found to be on their beds in the spring and early summer across New England, it is only sportsmanlike to release most of them taken at such times as the evidence is in this direction. The fun is in the strike, the action. "You can't eat a golfball and it's still a great game. Why not look at fishing in the same way—most of the time, at least?" This is often heard when experienced, thoughtful anglers get together.

It may be this attitude that is causing so many sportsmen to show preference for artificial lures and flies over baits. Nevertheless, as the weather and the water temperatures rise, bait fishing may be more effective, if less ethical, for both smallmouth and largemouth black bass.

Now, before somebody thinks I place more emphasis on returning smallmouths than largemouths to the water, especially in the spring during spawning periods, I must add that the largemouth spawns in northern waters during similar dates. Actually, largemouth spawn when the water temperatures reach 62°–65° Fahrenheit, and this means early May to late June. (Smallmouth bass require temperatures from 60°–70° Fahrenheit.)

Perhaps it is the rate of growth in the two kinds of bass that means more. Dependent on the amount and kind of feed, smallmouths may take three or four years to reach a length of nine inches. Where there is an abundance of suitable food, however, the smallmouth may reach that length by the second summer from birth. To reach trophy size, eighteen to twenty inches, smallmouths may have to live from seven to ten years, according to the available food and its growth qualities.

Meanwhile, largemouth bass may be eighteen or nineteen inches long by the time they are seven or eight years old. An eleven-inch largemouth might be in its third year. So, while there is fairly close similarity in the time it takes each to attain a given length, the largemouth will weigh appreciably more at any given age, where foods are available in equal amounts.

In Maine, there is a state-sponsored club to recognize trophy-sized fish. Only a few smallmouth bass reach the rigid requirement of five pounds for eligibility to the club but numerous largemouths qualify at the same weight, despite a much smaller population of largemouth bass in Maine. (Because many sportsmen are unable to tell the two kinds apart, distinction has not been made between largemouth and smallmouth bass; at least, up to this writing.)

Before I return to the uses of baits and artificials in shallow and surface-water fishing for bass, let me give a bit of information on weighty bass that may be surprising.

In a recent two-year state-sponsored contest in Massachusetts—rather than in a northern New England state—a twelve pound largemouth bass and a six-pound ten-ounce smallmouth were registered. In Connecticut, a seven-pound ten-ounce smallmouth bass earned an honor award in a national outdoor magazine contest (it came from Mashapaug Lake in Union) and a twelve-pound fourteen-ounce largemouth was the 1961 winner (northern division) in the same magazine's annual contest. The largemouth came from the same lake in Union, Connecticut.

I do not recall any largemouth bass of the size in these two southern New England states being entered in Maine's "One That Didn't Get Away Club," although I was in charge of this club for many years. Indeed, I would need to search the records to find smallmouths of weights similar to those mentioned above.

Personal experiences fishing in the comparatively few largemouth waters of Maine, nevertheless, proved exciting. Boosters of that state maintain that, in the colder waters "up north," all gamefish, including bass, fight harder than they do in more temperate environments. (Bass, in Maine, are found from an imaginary line drawn west to east across the state from below Rangeley near the New Hampshire border to south of Houlton on the Maine–New Brunswick boundary. So "up north" is relative to southern New England, not within Maine itself. Northern Maine is trout and salmon water, for the most part.)

So, then, here is something more specific on largemouth bass fishing as I have experienced it in Maine.

Author holds 4-lb largemouth taken on homemade streamer.

Some years ago, a good friend of mine, Llewellyn Colomy of Hallowell, Maine, was statewide president of the united sportsmen's clubs. He and I had frequent contacts because of my work for the state. He urged me to go bass fishing with him, in order that he might prove his claims of catching and releasing six-, seven- and occasionally eight-pound largemouths in a river and lake only eleven miles from my home in Augusta.

"We fish on the dark of the moon. The blacker the night, the better. Rainy weather and a new moon are a good combination," Lew told me.

Intrigued, since I knew he was an ardent conservationist and sportsman, I finally made a date with him. Another Maine outdoor writer, Gene Letourneau, who does a daily column for a chain of five newspapers, met us at a boat landing on the bank of Belgrade Stream.

The plan was this: We would motor across Messalonskee Lake, after going downstream a short distance, and have supper cooked out on a little island in the lake. Fishing wouldn't start until near midnight and we would be back at the boat livery on Belgrade Stream by daylight.

Well, a close friend of Lew's (Ray Lathe) was along to cook lobsters and clams, as well as to demonstrate their joint techniques in taking those husky largemouth bass.

Gene and I had our press cameras. The kind we used then was a heavy 4X5 Graphic. Thus, with our tackle and a piece of canvas I had brought to keep the cameras dry, our extra clothing, rainshirts, cooking utensils, axe, big tackle boxes, etc., the two boats were needed.

The seafood was better than that prepared by world famous chefs. (It was fresher, for one thing.) The mosquitoes weren't too hungry, at first. Conditions seemed ideal.

Then, just before dark, it began to rain. We hustled our gear under the canvas and donned rainshirts. But it rained torrents, so we four crawled under the canvas, hugging it around our shoulders, trying to keep the cameras reasonably dry and seeking to slant some of the rain off ourselves.

At times we dozed. Mostly, we laughed and wondered why—if I were to bring any kind of a shelter—I had to choose what actually was half a Scout pup tent, ancient, torn, weathered and barely waterproof.

By full darkness, we decided we might try the fishing.

"Couldn't be as uncomfortable as this."

Ray and Lew took compass bearings on the island and we agreed to stay close together in the two boats. It was blacker than the inside of a witch's heart. There were some swells on the lake but we followed Lew and Ray across a corner of the lake to a big weed patch near the mouth of Belgrade Stream, without incident.

Downeast bassland—old stumps in channel.

Lew told us: "We're going to fish with black Jitterbug plugs, using bait-casting rods. Our theory is, *the blacker the night, the blacker the lure.*"

Almost immediately, both Ray and Lew proved to Gene and me that they were experts in their favorite sport. I haven't seen faster fishing for anything except when I have cast streamer flies for ocean-going pollock during their surface schooling periods.

Gene and I tried for pictures. The boys would hold up largemouth in pairs—fish weighing, as they had promised, from six to eight pounds—and then snap a cigarette lighter so we could focus. But the rocking boats and the then inadequate lenses and film available meant we got few photos that were worth a hang.

Photographing the leaping, crazy-wild bass under the beam of a flashlight and with flashbulbs in our camera flashguns was an even more difficult task. We didn't get anything worthwhile. Nor would we ask Lew and Ray to keep any of their catch until daylight next morning. Lew had seen fishing go so far downhill in the mid-West that he had vowed not to save another gamefish so long as he lived.

The rain slackened. Fishing continued productive as, somehow, our models steered us to successive weed patches. However, they decided it would be hazardous to try to run back into Belgrade Stream until we had at least shadowy daylight to steer by.

Back on the little island, we rebuilt the fire and huddled around it until dawn. Chattering teeth, voracious mosquitoes and sticky clothing couldn't put down our enthusiasm for the bass action Gene and I had experienced.

Sometimes, on future visits, Lew and I fished during daylight hours in the little openings, streamside, formed by old stumps and weeds encircling small patches of water. I tossed streamer flies, Lew fished with both sinking and surface lures, mostly cast from his bait rods. Besides the Jitterbug, his favorite, a Crazy Crawler was effective in his fishing.

We lost more bass, due to the snarled cover, than we brought boatside. This didn't matter to either of us.

At no time, though, did the action approach that on the black, rainy night when we first fished together; unless and until we sought largemouths under similar conditions.

Variation of the bark raft to float a worm in stream currents, as we did in Vermont that time on the Missisquoi, was something I resorted to in the years that followed, when, in desperation over slow action, the unusual seemed indicated.

Variations like these—A nightcrawler hooked only on the head end, so the barb was buried in the worm and then fished by tossing the crawler onto lily pads, allowing it to rest there temporarily before I drew it lightly into the water beside the pads.—A pork-rind strip, fished in a similar way. —Poppers.—Even, occasionally, large dry flies, dropped onto rocks, pads and then floated in the same manner.

Many ardent anglers have experienced action when, inadvertently, they have "hung" a lure over a low tree limb and, in seeking to snap it free, have had it touch the water below and—*BANG*—have seen a bass hit with all of the primordial savagery so typical of this species. So, I have tried to perform this feat of piscatorial legerdemain purposely, as I am certain you have, on occasion. Usually, I have failed to (1) free the lure properly and therefore (2) have not been able to boat any bass that took the snarled offering. It's still fun to try, anyhow.

A more likely method for me is when I cast a spinning lure or popper side-arm and thus drop it in under low-hanging and water-shading tree limbs. Such darker patches of cover frequently harbor both largemouth and smallmouth bass. This seems especially so when the sun is high, hot and shining with merciless reflections on glassy-smooth water.

Variation in the kinds and speeds of retrieves of lures (and even of baits) sometimes has meant the difference between catching bass and not getting any response from them.

When both smallmouths and largemouths are on their spawning beds (in three to 22 feet of water, depending on water clarity for smallmouths and in twelve to 36 inches of water for largemouths) both kinds strike savagely, of course. They are highly protective of the nests, even if they may eat some of their offspring after hatching occurs!

If a lure is placed in proximity to the eggs, then, a bass will follow it as it moves away. In my experience, if I merely retrieve it by reeling or pulling the lure in steadily, strikes are not so apt to happen as when I take in line a few feet, stop the lure dead, then move it once more and continue to repeat this retrieving and stopping all the way to the boat or shore, as the case may be.

Most of my hits come when the lure has been moved and then stops. Bass seem to strike the motionless lure, instead of the moving one. But, again, they do want the lure to appear lively and not just be dropped into the water and left there. I fish it by starting my retrieve immediately after it sinks to what I believe to be nest depth; taking in a few feet, stopping it, and so on, as outlined above.

Another trick of mine, when fishing over nests or just any old time, involves the selection of a lure according to water clarity or discoloration. Just as my friend Lew Colomy decides the darker the night the blacker the lure, so I feel that the murkier the water, the darker my offering should be. When I can't see bottom in a few feet of water, I pick a black, brown or dark, colorless artificial from my kit. In clear, sparkling water, I find that a brightly hued lure or fly is effective. (More of this in a later chapter on the use of bucktails and streamer for bass fishing.)

Before we move on to the use of flies and poppers chiefly as bass enticers, though, let's look at still another way to fish for reluctant small-mouth and largemouth bass in New England waters.

Now, we must, with the following act of fish-fooling, have acceptable river or lake bottom; preferably sandy or rocky, at least hard clay. Not deep mud; not weedy to a considerable degree; not a bottom covered with old roots, tree limbs or with junk dumped there, unfortunately, by thoughtless individuals.

Given, then, reasonably good base under the water we are fishing, we may drop a sinking lure, like a small metal spoon, right onto the bottom. Then with our boat or canoe drifting slowly along in a mild breeze, we can bounce the artificial up and down as we drift, hitting the clay, sand or pebbles below and lifting the lure a few inches to create the bounces.

By drift fishing the entire lake according to the wind, we will often-times *discover* those shoals and feeding-hiding places so treasured by bass anglers. (I have marked particularly productive "hot spots" occasionally, so I would have them for future fishing in the same lake or river. I have done this by first sighting my location in two directions. I line up a tree with a church steeple, housetop, rock, or whatever is permanently visible and unusual enough to remember. Then I do the same in the opposite compass direction. By motoring out to the approximate spot, I then might find a inconspicuous marker: a tiny floating object, anchored with a piece of spare line and weight.)

In some of the lakes I fish for bass, as an example, I find weed patches below the surface during high water that occurs during rainy spells. These frequently have been located by the drift-fishing practice.

It is surprising, too, to have quite good action by bouncing a lure off the bottom, as I drift; or, when canoeing perhaps along a slow-moving, bassy stream in New England.

Other advantages of drift fishing off the bottom include a more inti-mate knowledge of where *not* to waste time on future trips, because of too deep water and similarly unfavorable conditions; where not to angle be-cause of snags; where not to run a motor too fast, since rocks lie just beneath the surface even far out from shore and safety.

This drifting and fishing can be done, I have found, when I am using baits and artificials in combination with baits. In this particular: I always remember that the "natural" foods of bass in New England include such items as hellgrammites, soft-shell crawfish, nightcrawlers, minnows; that they will, however, feed on little crustaceans, insects, frogs, mice, and almost anything else available.

My drift fishing in the East is largely with smallmouth rather than largemouth bass in mind—for largemouths like best the comparatively shallow, weed-grown areas (twenty feet and less deep.) They stay in such water because their food supply is there for the most part and because of the protection from sunken materials and aquatic growths. However, drift fishing has helped me to pinpoint such places in surprisingly unlikely locations, when lakes were much higher than normal.

I have had some luck in locating bass beds by catching bass when ice fishing for pickerel—even at times, when ice fishing for trout and salmon. Usually, laws require that bass be released by ice anglers but in certain places (read your law books to learn such spots) bass are legal quarry during ice-fishing seasons.

If bass have shown up, then, during periods of frozen water fishing, I have marked the areas mentally and have occasionally returned in summer to catch those bass released the winter before.

Often, too, other ice fishermen have told me where they have found bass during their forays for other fishes.

There are a few general thoughts to bear in mind if one is to have reasonably consistent success in bass fishing in New England, or elsewhere: First is the time of year when these fish are most likely to be active. In my experience, depending on the section of our region I am fishing, I prefer the early spring to early summer time (April–June, where legally open to fresh-water bass fishing) in southern New England; May to early July, according to regulations in each state in northern New England. (Vermont's bass season begins in average years at the time this is being written, the second Saturday in June; there is no closed season on smallmouth and largemouth bass in New Hampshire, again, at the time of this writing; and in Maine the season on single-hook artificial lures and flies begins June 1 and continues through June 20, when general use of lures and baits begins.)

During the summer months, with hot weather prevalent, I feel I have to resort to some of the out of the ordinary "tricks" referred to in this chapter; for bass are less apt to strike then, in shallow water, especially if the water temperatures are high and the sunshine bright.

From mid-August on into the fall, including October, where it is legal to fish for bass, I anticipate action often similar to that I enjoy in early spring. Perhaps, again, in shallow areas, near water weeds, old stumps, beside logs that have fallen into the lakes and rivers will I find my quarry.

And this leads us into whether to seek bass in deep water during hot weather; on rainy days, then; early in the morning or during evening and even after dark, when air and water temperatures make all life sleepy, indisposed to fight as strongly for existence. Or, whether to fish somewhat fruitlessly, I am afraid, during the height of the vacation season otherwise.

My youngest son Dale was told by several vacationers that there weren't any bass in Pocasset Lake, not far from his home. He went out a few hundred yards from shore in their boat, told them to anchor and drop baited lines over the side. In not time at all, they caught smallmouths of —to them—awesome size, despite the fact that they had fished fruitlessly for a week until then.

Blessed with fishing and hunting "for a living," since I write about these sports in my chosen field of work, still I have found myself in the predicament of those vacationers far too often not to seek the advice of a local sportsman or guide, regardless of location. A good guide for a day or two, at least, is worth whatever his fee may be. All I can tell you and everything you may read and study about New England bass fishing otherwise may not put bass on your stringer, without specific knowledge of *where* precisely to place your lures the kinds of offerings you should make at any given time and situation.

If you don't find bass to fish over, acting on the advice of a knowledgeable local resident, then you will at the very least have a chance to say: "Guide didn't know his business. That's why I can't show you any bass today."

There are good and poor guides, of course. As a general rule, though, anybody willing to earn a living sitting in an open boat for hours on end, without a helmet and safety goggles to guard his head and eyes against your gang hooks, his life dependent on whether or not you get careless and upset the canoe, too, should at least be cited for bravery, strength and normally for a genuine New England sense of humor that can soften your unhappiness if you fail to catch fish and/or when you write out the check for the day's entertainment and search.

So, to fly fishing next—a specialized kind of bass fishing sport that gives you and me an "out" every time we seek wary New England bronzebacks. If we aren't successful, we always say: "I put them all back, as I always do."

Smallmouth jumps close to boat.

3

FLY FISHING FOR BASS

Fly fishing for black bass in New England can be enjoyable, often productive, and an ethical, high-level sport. While it is, as previously written in this book, fastest when the smallmouth and largemouth are on their spawning beds, actually that precise period is so comparatively brief—and location of beds so indefinite—as to limit any kind of fishing definitude for the average bass angler.

So, on the whole and for most bass seekers, our discussion of fly fishing for this species must include the "off" as well as the exceptional "on" target times.

How, then, is it done in a reasonably effective way?

Since bucktail flies and poppers, as well as certain other flyrod artificials, are bulky, wind resistance is appreciable. This means that tackle should be heavy enough to use under somewhat adverse conditions. I suggest the following:

At least an 8 ft. flyrod; preferably 8 ft. 6 in. and, if you can handle a longer one (9 ft., for instance) so much the better. (The way to avoid fatigue and sore muscles is not to "overcast." By this I mean make each cast count by fishing your fly all the way back to the boat or canoe. Do not merely try for distance, then pick up your fly and make repeated casts. Fish don't hit in the air, remember, but on or in the water. False casting isn't so necessary to achieve distance, either, when the rod is long enough to carry the bulky fly to its target.)

As to the make of rod, like everything else, usually the more it costs the better it performs. Many tonkin cane rods manufactured today have stiff action and are conceived for the delicate dry flies we use to entice trout and salmon. This is especially true of rods up to and including the 7 ft. 6 in. lengths. (Here is another reason for fishing with at least an eight-footer when heavy bass artificials are being cast.) The shorter trout rods have what one manufacturer calls "super light, accurate dry fly action." Hardy's cane-built fly rods in 8 ft. 6 in. and the 8 ft. one, too, have "medium action, for either dry or wet fly fishing."

Grand Lake Stream, Maine guide Ken Butts holds a 3¾ lbs smallmouth caught by author on Hardy rod.

As I mentioned in the Introduction my choice for bass presently is a Hardy 8 ft. 6 in. Palakona cane rod. It is designed to handle dry, wet, streamer flies and bass bugs with what the maker terms "equal ease and accuracy."

I use it with an AFTM No. 8 line—forward or bug taper (the former when fishing wet and the bug taper for poppers and outsize dry patterns). The reasoning behind the difference in lines is to favor the rod a bit when I lift a sinking line from beneath, instead of off, the water. There is considerable drag to a wet line and I don't want to put a set in a medium-action, more limber rod. In some lines, at least, the shooting taper part of the line is of heavier diameter in a bug taper than in a regular forward taper.

With a bit of practice, anybody can learn to take advantage of the motion imparted to a medium- or soft-action flyrod when casting a line that fits the cane. Then, rather than "heaving" the line out from a stiff "stick," we can get distance not only from the line but from the extra push of the limber, swaying flyrod itself. Just as a sprung bow projects an arrow, so a soft-action flyrod adds velocity to a line and helps us achieve distance with less energy.

Were I six feet and more tall, I might prefer to use a rod like Hardy's No. 9 Jet Set fiberglass, medium powerful flyrod. It is 9 ft. long and weighs 5 ¼ ounces. The rod casts a No. 9 line well. Built for strippers, steelheads and sea-run salmon, it is also effective for fresh-water bass. (A two-inch extension handle is hardly necessary for our New England largemouths and smallmouths, of course, but this does convert it to multiple uses.)

The cost of the "Fibalite" rod is about $35 less than the Palakona cane, which might well make a difference in an individual choice.

The reels suggested for these rods by Hardy are Saint Aidan for the 8 ft. 6 in. cane, and Husky for the 9 ft. fiberglass rod. The former can be purchased in regular or as a multiplier reel. The Husky has a brake mechanism that lessens the need to use its full power and to assure that it wears indefinitely.

Either of the reels above will take all the line and backing necessary for bass fishing and, indeed, for all-'round use when other species are sought.

Besides Hardy, there are many other fine rods and reels on the market —made in this country and abroad, of course. Properly cared for, quality tackle need not be expensive when considered as a lifetime investment, even as something to be willed to successive generations. It hardly depreciates in value—may even be worth more as time goes on.

Attached to my fly lines are tapered leaders of about the same length as the rod; in the case of the 8 ½ ft. cane, a 9 ft. leader. I prefer the tippet to run about 6 lbs. test—not for its strength especially, but so I may cast bulky lures and flies more readily when the wind blows.

Gusty days, particularly those when we have what riflemen call "fishtail winds" (those that change direction frequently) make casting not only difficult but can endanger a second person in a boat. Seated in the bow of a canoe or rowboat, with a companion or guide paddling or running a motor slowly in the stern, a caster, I have found, can whip a flyrod sidewise and nearly horizontal to the water. By this method and by casting out across the bow—instead of allowing the rod tip and consequently the popper or fly to drift astern—I can avoid hooking my stern man.

Another method is to straddle the bow seat side-to my companion and facing the shoreline. According to whether one is right- or left-handed, he needs to turn completely around to face the shore, of course, when the boat is running in a direction contrary to the way he is seated. And, again, he should cast out over the bow, not back.

Any angler who has been hooked, or who has impaled a friend on a bass bug or fly, has learned the hard way what just isn't done out fishing.

The longer rod, even fished vertically, keeps a barb higher in the air.

To be disputatious, I might vow that the effectiveness of a streamer or bucktail fly is superior to that of a bass popping bug. However, I won't argue the case, only say that personally I catch more bass with flies than with poppers. Admittedly, I fish more for smallmouth bass, in my opinion, a deeper feeder on the whole than the largemouth. When I fish for largemouth, I am partial to a surface lure much of the time and the bugs then produce fish very well.

A further admission: Bass fishermen who live in the largemouth country often become more proficient in the use of poppers, artificial frogs, hair mice and the like, than I ever have become by neglecting to use these artificials to anywhere near the extent that I cast flies. The lures you and I use most naturally catch the most bass—for us.

So, on a recent trip Downeast, with *Field & Stream* Executive Editor Al McClane, Al could and did take smallmouth bass on a variety of flies and poppers. I caught all of my bass on streamers and bucktails.

Now, for many years I have used the larger sizes for bass but in at least one lake in the Grand Lake Stream section I found that a No. 10 Mickey Finn, *not* a No. 2 on long shank hook, was much more productive. Thus are lifelong theories and seemingly proven experiences suddenly disproven. The large size bucktails sank faster and thus got down sooner and deeper—I always theorized—to where the smallmouths would be lying in wait. Not only that, but *larger lures for larger fish of any kind* was another of my firm beliefs.

When I took only a few bass in Keg Lake, then, my guide said, in the apologetic way that Downeasters mention an obvious fact: "Bass seem to hit a smaller fly here. Try this little Mickey. It's been good, especially in this lake."

The water was clear, so at least my theory of the greater the water clarity the lighter color the fly should be, was borne out.

Grudgingly, with mumbled thanks, I switched to his No. 10 yellow and white hair bucktail. Casting in toward a rocky shore, I allowed the line to take the fly down fairly deep. Then, as I had been doing, I brought it back toward the boat with short, fast retrieves and brief stops here and there.

The guide was watching the fly. "Nice one followed it!" he exclaimed.

I, too, saw a dark shadow turn sharply away from the boat side. Casting again, I slowed my retrieves and let the Mickey Finn rest a bit longer on those in-between stops. Now I jiggled my rod tip to seemingly bring the fly to life, then pulled quickly on the line, to suggest to any waiting bass that this odd minnow was going to escape if he didn't grab it in a hurry.

The line drew back, burning through the skin of my fingers. The rod bowed. The reel whined in protest. Water split wide open to allow passage for a beautiful bass, as it surfaced and continued up into the air like a jumping duck.

"Wow!" It's a big one!"

The guide was as thrilled as if this were his first bass, instead of literally the thousands he must have seen performing similar, crazy antics.

My camera was around my neck. I lowered the rod tip and handed the butt end to the guide. "Play him," I urged, "I want to get pictures of him jumping."

The bass was highly cooperative in this regard. He jumped three times more and, satisfied that he was on film for posterity, I took back the rod and brought the smallmouth slowly to net. He fought valiantly all the way. As the guide slipped the net toward him, he leaped into the air once again, almost landing in the boat.

"Wow!" It was my turn to shout in awe and admiration for such strength and tenacity as the bass possessed.

We weighed him—3 ¾ pounds. Easing him into the lake, belly down, we watched as his gills moved in and out steadily then sighed as, with a flip of his tail, he swam off in well deserved freedom.

The little Mickey Finn produced a succession of bass all morning long. Al McClane and his guide were fishing in another part of the lake. When we joined them at a lunch-ground site later, Al was busily photographing a pair of big smallmouths for his magazine and widely recognized *Standard Fishing Encyclopedia,* new edition.

Author poses with pair of fat bass.

I learned that Al had been fishing much of the time with a kind of pinkish-white imitation shrimp pattern on a No. 8 long-shank hook. Casting similarly to the way I had, he had brought to net about the same number of smallmouths, he told me. The fly Al had been casting would sink faster than my small Mickey Finn, for it was heavier. So he could get it over bass in a few seconds less, perhaps.

Anyhow, this proved that it wasn't the little Mickey that those Keg Lake smallmouth wanted exclusively.

Once, a year or two before, I had fished for bass with Lionel "Lal" Lemieux, a newspaperman from Lewiston, Maine. We were "covering" a trip Downeast by Ed Dodd and a friend of his on that occasion.

Smallmouth had proved much more reluctant to strike than when I fished with McClane. Finally, I bent on a big, bushy orange and yellow streamer fly (hook size No. 2), and made a cast against a high sandy bank, allowing my wet fly line to carry the streamer all the way to bottom. After it had rested there a while, I started my usual retrieve and on about the third haul-and-stop-the-fly, I had a vicious strike. True to form in cold-water lakes (this one was Scraggley in Washington County, Maine) the bass surfaced explosively, skittered along on its tail, dove and jumped into the air repeatedly. The excitement of both men in a boat on such an occasion is mutually shared. Lal was as breathless as I, I'm certain.

Later, I took a few other smallmouths with the same fly, fished in precisely the same manner. The depth of those "holes" in which bass were lying that day was much greater than that in which I usually find smallmouths. It was later in the season (mid-July) and weather was warm. So, apparently, fish were seeking cooler depths.

Back at the lunch-ground with Al McClane, I was remembering how the man who had been guiding Al all morning had prepared my bass and cooked them, when Lal and I joined Ed Dodd and his party on that earlier fishing trip.

I started to suggest that Les Williams and Ken Butts (Al's and my guides) cook up a couple of the larger smallmouths in the same manner. They were 'way ahead of me. The fire was burning briskly and a huge iron frypan with a handle a yard long (literally) contained cooking oil that was boiling and bubbling by the time the two guides dropped into it thick fillets of freshly caught bass.

The fish soon were golden brown. Al and I picked up chunks of bass from paper plates and ate it with our fingers, murmuring between bites "Man, is that ever delicious!"

That afternoon, between Les Williams' and Ken Butts' familiarity with the lake and McClane's knowledge of what constitutes "good" bass water (Al is a graduate fisheries biologist and he can "read" bass habitat like a book) we continued to hit, play and release smallmouths consistently.

Next morning, Al wanted to check out a lake that is accessible by car, with a launching site and picnic area right on the shore. He wanted to see what fishing pressure had done to Clifford Lake since he last had fished it years before. (Clifford is southwest of Big Lake and the town of Princeton.)

"There used to be big bass in Clifford, then. But they weren't over the entire lake, just in certain spots," Al recalled.

"Better for pickerel," one of our guides said. "It's ice-fished quite a lot in winter."

We arrived at Clifford the following day, regardless. I elected to "shoot" pictures. Al's first fish was a big eastern chain pickerel. He suggested that the guide cruise the shoreline until Al indicated where to stop in what logically should be bass habitat. He picked the spots with amazing regularity from then on. Every time Al said: "Let's fish here," he struck smallmouths. Not so many as we had played the day before at Keg Lake but enough to make the fishing interesting. The bass ran a couple of pounds and more. They were beautiful fish, somewhat lighter in color than those at Keg.

But, what do we do to locate bass when an Al McClane and an experienced guide are not available?

First of all, thinking of that peak fishing during their spawning time, we must decide to choose one of the New England states that has an open season during that rather brief period when bass are on their beds in average years.

We have indicated that this is the first 20 days in June in Maine. In New Hampshire—at least at this writing—there are no closed seasons, weight or length limits on either largemouth or smallmouth bass. The daily count limit is five bass allowable per fisherman. The spawning time should be similar to that in Maine, allowing for the difference in temperatures of water along the southern fringe of lakes and rivers and of those in the northern mountain section.

In Vermont, the current open season on both largemouth and smallmouth bass begins the second Saturday in June. Bass may be on their beds in northerly areas of the state as late as mid-June but it is assumed that, as used to be the case in New Hampshire years ago, the opening date is deferred to protect bass during their spawning periods.

In Massachusetts, the season on most gamefishes, including bass, begins the third Saturday in April. So, the chances of finding bass on their beds (probably during May) are good.

In Rhode Island, the season opens on both largemouths and small-mouths April 18 and, again, the chances of finding bass spawning (perhaps as early as late April but more likely during May) are good.

Finally, Connecticut has a season from April 15 to March 31 for both smallmouth and largemouth bass. Thus, ice fishing for bass also is a legal method there. In most of the bass waters, spawning should begin in May, or earlier.

Regardless of the emphasis I might place on hitting bass on their spawning beds for faster than usual action, there are at least two factors to keep in mind: First, that the spawning period actually is brief at best. According to water temperatures, largemouth bass may hatch from eggs within a week or ten days—if the water is 65° Fahrenheit. If it is 80° the eggs may hatch as quickly as in five days. So, this doesn't give us too much leeway in hitting that peak of fishing then.

Nor do smallmouths give us any better break. It takes from as little as two days and hardly more than nine for eggs to incubate, according to water temperatures.

When we do find bass on their beds, it is well to remember that largemouth spawn in water from a foot to as much as three feet in depth. Nests usually are only seven or eight feet from shore, however. So we have to put our lures nearly on the banking at this time and draw them out just a short way to stir the guardians of their nests.

Insofar as smallmouth nests are concerned, these are located as a rule in from three to 22 feet of water. The better water clarity the deeper the nests lie, again, in general. The distance from shore may, then, be roughly judged by the depth of water and whether it is muddy or clear, most of the time.

Renowned fishing editor Al McClane holds a big Maine chain pickerel, caught incidental to bass.

A thermometer reading can give a fisherman some idea of approximate times either largemouths or smallmouths may be on their beds. Until water attains at least 62° for largemouths and 60° for smallmouth bass, it is apparent nothing much is hatching down below.

Second, a factor I like to emphasize is the value to all of us of returning to the water bass hooked and played during the spawning times. Unless the wind is blowing a mild gale, it seems to me, bass will find their way back to the beds when released. If the craft drifts a long distance before the hooked fish can be brought in and freed, the fish may not relocate his identical spawning site, I suspect. Anyhow, a fish saved then should be valuable as an investment in future fishing. A largemouth male fish guards the nest and even the young offspring for a short time after they hatch.

If a ripe female bass is caught, her release means that as many as 2,000 to 7,000 eggs per pound of body weight goes with her. All eggs do not ripen simultaneously, of course.

Especially in northern New England waters, experience proves a wide variation in when bass spawn. This means that I select, if time permits in any given area, a section that has a considerable number of lakes, streams, and rivers where water temperatures may vary appreciably.

In this regard, it is good to establish local contacts in places where bass fishing is dependable. Just as a skier can save himself from driving miles to a snowless slope—traveling instead to one where reports indicate good skiing—so can a bass angler choose those waters in which bass are reported active because water temperature is ideal at the moment. Local sportsmen and guides can tell us what to anticipate. It's kind of a *save now* (on fishing time) *and spend* (more time) *later* idea.

In spite of the foregoing, most of our days spent fishing for bass will be enjoyed at other than spawning times. How, then, do we "read" shore-line and water signs that tell us—not as accurately as Al McClane interprets them but, at least in a general way, so we don't waste precious hours fruitlessly—that *here there are bass?*

For largemouth, I emphasize that this bass likes comparatively shallow water, with weeds growing lushly for his food and protection. They hardly ever stray too far from vegetation that harbors insects, crawfish, frogs and smaller fish on all of which they like to feed. They eat more in warmer spring weather than during late fall and winter.

Smallmouth bass, on the other hand, seem to do quite well in comparatively large lakes, as well as in cool-water ponds and rivers. Gravel bars that cut apart bottom growths of weeds are likely spots. Bass may lie in as much as twenty feet of water; perhaps even more, when such conditions are found.

I noticed, too, that McClane was quick to spot rocky hillsides dropping down into the Maine lakes we fished together. And that he didn't pass up trying his luck on points of land that run out into some of the lakes—particularly when the points were gravelly and rocky looking.

As mentioned earlier, a fish finder is a logical piece of equipment, unless and until we are very familiar with any given piece of water. Those shallow bars of gravel or sand, often lying well out in lakes and ponds, almost certainly will harbor smallmouth bass, since they frequent these shoals to feed on small minnows, crawfish and similar, appealing (to them), items of their diet.

Thus, I find out if I am visiting largemouth water or if the prevalent species is the smallmouth bass. From the foregoing it can be seen that the habitat and food areas of the two fishes are quite different in northern New England.

In time, instinct tells a fisherman almost precisely where to fish in a lake and which spots to pass up in favor of more promising areas.

Another way, too, which doesn't take all day, now that we are in the age of the outboard motor, is to occasionally drop a lure over the stern of a boat and then circle a lake slowly, keeping fifteen or twenty yards off and parallel with the shoreline until a bass strikes. If lucky, that section should be "worked" with fly casting. (See Chapter 2 on see-sawing a boat while trolling.)

In Chapter 1 I suggested that both kinds of bass, in my opinion, sometimes lie adjacent to their feeding "grounds" but in quite deep water—coming up onto the shelves to catch their food and then dropping down into the cool, deep holes to rest and act lazy. This occurs particularly in hot, mid-summertime and in those waters in southern New England that reach higher temperatures ideal for bass.

Personally, then, I never hesitate to experiment but I don't do it so often nor so long that the common-sense ideas and experience I have tried to outline above are lost in the shuffle of originality.

Bass, even more than people, are creatures of habit. I seek to learn those practices which are somewhat common to these fish and to profit by such piscatorial know-how. We all find out tricks of the sport by fishing, by reading what the so-called "experts" have to say, and finally by listening to our friends, guides and fish professionals in their discussions of our Number One gamefish in this nation (in inland waters, that is).

I just don't believe that we can learn as much in a month, even in a year, from all other sources except actual fishing experience, despite all suggestions. This is particularly true of fly fishing for bass, in my opinion.

Consider, if you will, how I learned the hard way that smallmouths in turbid water wanted a dark fly, that those in clear water seemed to hit a bright colored fly much more often. It had to be a question of trial and error. Any angler knows that he isn't convinced until it is indisputable that such seemingly irrelevant facts fit into his fishing picture.

So, many years ago, I fished for bass in New Hampshire and in Maine rather haphazardly, trying this pattern and that one, sometimes having pretty good catches and at other times getting skunked.

Perhaps it was Lew Colomy's theory that largemouths decide *the darker the night, the blacker the lure,* as I wrote earlier, that hit me in the head with the thought that smallmouths, too, might see a dark fly in roily water better than they could spot a light one. Perhaps, it was just that I had one of those days when bass were coming so fast on a black bucktail that I experimented with light colors and failed to keep up the pace. Anyhow, I found out something that I swear by myself. I believe it will work for you, too.

Whatever the experience or reasoning that convinced me, how often I have fished in central Maine in Maranacook Lake (upper end near the town of Readfield) and cast a dark brown or coal black deer hair pattern on a No. 2 or 4 streamer hook and had hit after savage hit by nesting bass in the years gone by. (Recent visits there have left me wondering if the bass have gone from that location. There are numerous cottages on that section of Maranacook now and in a few hours of fishing I failed to take a bass.)

Yet, how often, too, have I used a red and white bucktail, a Mickey Finn, a self-conceived yellow and orange streamer in the clear waters Downeast, usually with great and convincing success.

Small items of fishing lore, garnered through the years, add up and make sense to me now. Again, this knowledge, such as it is, has come to me mostly from personal experience, from actual fishing trips, from getting out and going where the bass live and then from fishing long hours every day.

It was a relative of mine who expressed it this way, when I wondered why we don't get as many fish as we used to. He said: "Most people oversleep in the morning when the bass are active, and they come ashore for cocktails and dinner in the evening, about the time bass start to hit again any given day. If you want a fish, you have to stay with them and do things in a *fishmanlike* manner."

Maine guide Les Williams steps ashore with a duo of bass.

Female largemouth black bass. (top)
Female smallmouth black bass. (bottom)

Belgrade Stream in central Maine is good fishing for both large and smallmouth bass. Dale Elliot, N. Wayne, Maine is shown above with a catch.

Bordering Maine but largely in New Hampshire, Province Lake is often productive of smallmouth bass.

Torsey Pond, Readfield–Mt. Vernon, Maine yields fat black bass. Author uses large flies, such as those shown in his fishing hat, when seeking smallmouths there.

St. Croix River and its West Branch (Maine–New Brunswick section) is ideal habitat for smallmouth bass.

Dale Elliot of N. Wayne, Maine comes ashore at Pocasset Lake, Wayne, after a successful fishing foray.

Belgrade Lakes, Maine has miles of good bass water.   Long Pond lies near Great, North, East and Messalonskee Lakes—all excellent bass habitat.

Pools in warm-water New England streams usually hold black bass.

Bass flies: Upper, *Gray Ghost no. 2 hook;* center, *small Mickey Finn, no. 8 hook;* bottom, *author's design, No. 2 hook, with orange and yellow body and wings. Note that wings extend well beyond the barb.*

Curved hook shank for action. Gray wool body with hair tied in as in Palmer Fly No. 8, short-shank hook.

Other bass flies: two upper, *No. 4 Brown Wulff and No. 4 Wulff with cropped body for better flotation. Lower left, Big Salmon River (New Brunswick) pattern for Atlantic, sea-run salmon. No. 4 hook. Floats well and produces bass. Right is wet fly tied by Rogan of Donegal, Ireland. The pattern is called Bull Dog no. 6 hook.*

Typical cork-bodied bass popper. Comes in wide range of sizes and one of better top-water flyrod lures.

Floating flyrod lure. About no. 6 hook. Cropped wool with coarse nylon "feelers." Can be adapted to one's own preference by adding more streamers of nylon.

Spinning and/or spin-casting lures.

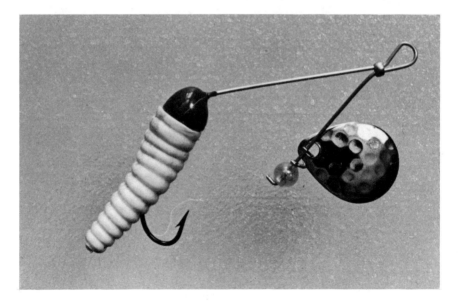

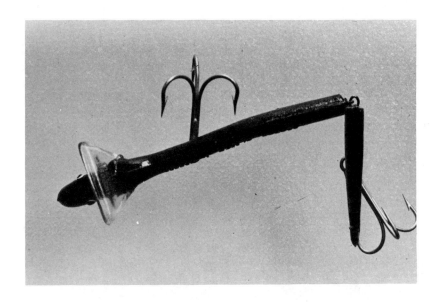

Spinning and/or spin-casting lure.

Productive fishing plug. According to size, can be plug-cast from baitrod rig, spin-cast, trolled.

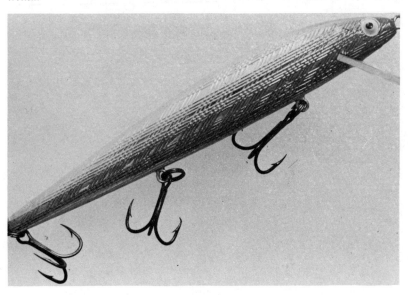

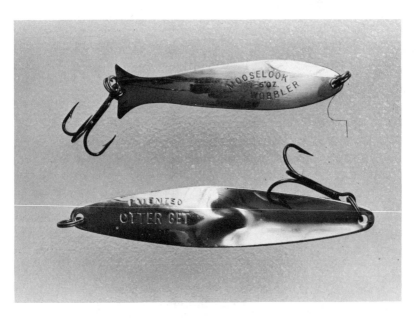

Two New England favorites for all gamefish, including black bass. According to size can be spin-cast, baitrod cast, trolled, jigged (where legal). Smaller sizes even can be used fly fishing with wet line.

4

FURTHER FLYROD FISHING

Despite my admission that I use streamer flies more by far than I cast poppers and other surface artificials, especially for smallmouth bass, I do on occasion find bass-bugging with a flyrod provides faster action than I experience at the time with only streamers, fished on a wet flyline.

And (see Chapter 3) I never overlook surface lures when largemouth bass are being sought in New England waters.

If my readers get as much of a kick out of catching bass on self-conceived "floaters" and "sinkers" as I do, then they will understand one of the reasons, at least, that I spend an appreciable amount of time tying up flies to imitate small frogs, mice, bees and butterflies; why I have thought of and whittled out surface lures from such unlikely things as old-fashioned clothespins, cedar shingles, etc. Yet, I must admit that commercially manufactured lures usually beat mine "all hollow"—not only in being easier to cast but in producing more strikes. Still, I keep on tying and trying. Don't we all?

I have had some luck fishing a fly of unique design. Taking a No. 4 streamer hook, I lash a crosspiece behind the eye a short distance, leaving room enough to tie on a head, as is usual on any fly.

Now, I wind hackle feathers around and around the crosspiece (this cross wire is just a short section of a paper clip). Then, I wind on hackle feathers lengthwise along the hook shank. The feathers usually are white, since my idea is to imitate a white miller moth with this fly.

Dressing the pattern often and thoroughly with the same spray used to float any dry fly ("UP" is one kind manufactured commercially), we note that the "moth" floats fairly well. It is tough to cast if the wind blows but moths aren't in evidence in windy weather, anyway.

Without any sort of body dressing to weight the contraption further, the bare hook, cross wire and hackle feathers are light and airy.

An old recipe used to float flies and other surface lures is made from melted paraffin stirred into carbon tetrachloride (the noninflammable solvent used in cleaning mixtures and as a fire extinguisher liquid). *Don't heat the carbon tet;* just soften the paraffin wax enough to stir the two together. Kept in a small, hand-sized jar, it can be warmed by holding it between the palms of one's hands for a minute or two. When the mixture strikes the water, the wax hardens and keeps a floater afloat quite satisfactorily.

With all of the low-cost sprays on the market, we wonder why we bother with such gunky solutions, but it does work.

Insofar as the white miller artificial I tie occasionally, it admittedly doesn't cast as easily as a No. 4 White Wulff salmon fly; nor can I state categorically that I can catch any more bass on my creation. The big Wulff is close enough to a natural moth to take even choosy trout, so why should bass be finicky?

Furthermore, almost any commercial floater looks better than a stubby, sawed-off clothespin with a hook screwed into the tail. I paint such homemade "bugs" and sometimes attach a porkrind strip to the hook. Maybe it's my thought that "if this catches bass, anything will, and I can prove they're in here, anyhow."

Now, using porkrinds, it is obviously much easier to create bass teasers than it is to fashion flies or plugs. For one thing, I can attach my own design to a proven spinner or floating plug that has enticed bass previously. Then, I can assume partial credit, at least!

Fished on a bare hook, the homemade porkrind designs have to have something going for them, of course. And pickerel love pork strips so much that a bass has to fight his way to any such "bait" at times.

But, like you, I experiment with old spoons, sometimes soldering hooks to them and breaking off the stem; at other times just drilling a hole so I can attach a ring for the hook. Finally, drilling a hole in the "head" of the spoon for a swivel, to which I can attach my line or leader—depending on whether I am spinning or fly fishing.

I could go on and on.

What truly are the benefits of these homemade artificials? Not in the money saved, nor usually in the fish-taking qualities; rather, they are conversation pieces. Frequently, we tie bass flies as members of a club and create other lures with similar groups. When winter closes us in, here in New England, our enthusiasm is maintained by such activities.

Indeed, particularly when artificial flies are considered, tying them becomes as important as actual fishing, to many sportsmen. This is indeed an entirely separate hobby. Like you, I know some men who rarely go fishing but who tie beautiful flies that will take bass consistently. Not so many in my acquaintance "build" other lures, yet many do so, regardless.

And, we all "discover" methods of fishing our own and commercial flies and lures effective when bass hit well.

Once I fished with a guide named "Artie" MacKenzie. He experimented almost constantly. His tackle boxes were as large as small suitcases and they held one of the widest assortment of flies, plugs, spoons, spinners, jigs and poppers that I ever saw anywhere except in a tackle shop.

Artie would fish a lure for a few minutes and if he didn't get a strike he would change to something else.

"Fish get tired of looking at the same old thing," he told me. "Many sportsmen catch a bass on a certain lure, so they decide that it is the one to use indefinitely. Not me. I believe in change."

Artie rarely got skunked, so doubtless he had something there. Maybe his strongest attribute, however, was a thorough knowledge of where fish would be lying or feeding at any specific hour of the day and in all of the waters within fishing distance of his home. Also, he had learned *how* to offer a lure to bass to encourage them to hit.

Now, this is actually something every man must find out for himself, in my opinion. Certain authorities will urge us to place a fly or surface popper as gently as possible on the water. Then, move it enough to attract the attention of bass but not so violently as to frighten the bass and cause them to swim hurriedly for shelter. Others describe the fast fishing that results from slamming a plug onto the water. It's like the old gag about the skinner who said you have to hit a mule hard to get his attention and then you could use him gently.

I like to try different ways, keeping all options open. If I drop a big dry fly or popper gently on the water, where past experience has shown bass should be lying, and if I move it lightly and plop-plop it easily and still don't get action, I'll try this method a few more times. Then, gradually, I'll increase the tempo until I have quite a disturbance going. If neither method works, then I'll go on to another logical place for bass and try an entirely different pattern of fly or design of bug, pork strip, hair mouse or floating frog and, again, fish these offerings gently at first, but more roughly if I think it may bring hits from the reluctant bronzebacks.

Once a method is established on any given occasion and in any specific period—both of which can be deciding factors, I believe—then I will adopt that way of fishing for the time being.

It does appear to me that there are days when bass are guarding their beds, for example, and when nearly anything that falls on the surface above them—or sinks down near their eggs—will cause them to smash such objects. Again, there are times when the bass are lethargic from hot weather or for other reasons, and it takes a small earthquake to arouse them. If anglers were precise enough to keep their experiences in day-by-day diaries, they might refer back and quickly find the answer in one section or another. Yet, who wants to fish by computer? Each trip should be a challenge for us to outwit the smallmouth or largemouth bass; not a predetermined, assured plot to bring home legal limits.

Another ancient quip states that *fish have one of the smaller brains of any living organism, but a great many so-called intellectual humans spend a lifetime trying to outthink them.* So, that's what I'm doing; and, I've got even more strikes against me, because nobody ever has called me an 'intellectual.'

Bass near rock is on terminal tackle of the late Joe Brooks, nationally famous writer.

I emphasize experimentation when bass fishing because of the tricks that have paid off for me personally, or for others who have told me about unusual results from their own unique, *try-anything-when-desperate* approaches. For example:

Last August I visited one of my sons and his family while they were camping in Norway, Maine. The campground is on Sand Pond, where there is neither size nor bag limit on pickerel and bass. Neil had several good-sized smallmouths on ice. I helped him fillet them so our wives could make a fish chowder. This gave us merit points to use up fishing together that evening.

He set up a combination fly- and spin-rod of just a bit over two ounces in weight. As we stepped into his small car-top boat, I commented that I favor a much heavier, longer cane rod for bass fishing. Neil smiled.

"Last night, I began casting with a glass rod and bass poppers. Didn't get any action. I used a variety of big flies and still didn't raise a bass.

"I kept noticing a hatch of tiny flies on the water and once in a while fish would suck them in—not come up and smash the insects but just pull them down in a kind of soft rise that left only a dimpling ring on the surface.

"I figured they were small bass, or sunfish, but I wasn't getting any action so I set up my little rod here and put on this fly."

He showed me a little No. 14 Dark Hendrickson dry fly.

Noticing my incredulous look, Neil continued:

"I must have caught and released 50 smallmouths and I kept those we filleted, a couple of which, as you must have noticed, were in the two pound or so class."

"You mean bass that size took a No. 14 dry fly?"

Neil grinned. "You should have seen the one I lost. It must have weighed four pounds. Had it on for a quarter of an hour and more. The leader held but I suppose the bass was lightly hooked and the tiny barb worked free.

"Sure hated to lose that one!"

As we talked, we were moving slowly along in the boat with Neil at the oars. In shallow water, he made a cast or two, dropping the pinned-in oars from time to time, to do so. Nearly every time his tiny dry fly hit the water a little bass or a sunfish would take it. On his tonkin cane flyrod, they gave him good, if brief action.

Following his style, I bent on a 14 Cooper's Bug—a deer-hair floater. It was gray and brown. I caught fish the same size as Neil was bringing to net.

He said, "This is the cove where a camping neighbor of mine caught a smallmouth of 3-¾ pounds, just last evening. Bass have been hitting well most of this week. He was using small poppers."

As often happens, when a fisherman wants most to prove a point, neither Neil nor I took any big bass that evening. The preliminary hatch consisted of those black, hair-like skaters that flick over the water of lakes at times. None of the tiny moths or flies that Neil had imitated the evening before showed when I fished with him. He wondered why.

"The weather is about ten degrees cooler than it has been for the past several days, Neil. It looks like rain. There's a bit of wind stirring outside these sheltered coves, I've noticed."

We fished on, as gathering shadows spread across the lake, hoping that the smallmouths would become active.

Using my heavier tackle, I tried a much larger pattern of fly that, when dressed with silicone "UP," floated well enough. It was on a No. 8 streamer hook and it plopped when I twitched the rod.

Then, I accepted a little popper from Neil. It was cork-bodied but very small and sported a few tail feathers. The head was black and white and it was cupped slightly.

I said: "There's a rising fish of some kind."

The circle had dimpled much farther from shore than we had been fishing. I made a long cast. The second the popper struck the water, a broad black back arced over the lure but there was too much slack in the line for me to strike quickly enough.

"That was a beauty!"

I cast in the same area once more. A small bass took the popper at once. I brought it in, muttering:

"That's not the same fish, at all."

We kept trying until full darkness set in; took a few more smallmouths about five and six inches long, but none worth talking about.

On the way to shore, we saw bass fishermen using bait, poppers, plugs —the works. Their fishing had been even slower than ours; for Neil's tiny dry flies had at least been effective for undersized fish.

I told my son: "Neil, in all of the years I've fished for bass, it never occurred to me to use trout tackle for them. Never mind if we didn't do well this evening. I've learned a trick from your experience that not only may save me from going fish-less on future bass trips but one that will give me more fun than I ever thought possible.

"I'll have my two-ounce Hardy with me from now on, as well as this 8½-footer. And a book of dry flies besides."

Neil said, "Nobody believed me when I told them yesterday that I caught those bass on a No. 14 dry fly. You'll have to show other bass fishermen that this trick will really work before they'll believe you, too."

"Maybe some of them already fish with dries in the smaller sizes, for all I know. I haven't seen them doing so. Nor, again, have I ever thought of trout tackle for bass until now.

"Could be we're 'way behind the times. Nothing new under the sun, they say."

Neil quipped, "But, when the sun is shining this wouldn't work. It's an evening hatch switch; or, maybe a trick to try when bass are feeding at night, early in the morning, or on dark, cloudy days."

I recalled that I had often fished for white perch and other panfish with a fly and had great fun and frequently fast action. And, of course, had used larger sizes of dry flies, as well as streamers and bucktails, for New England bass. Why hadn't I, in all of my years of bass fishing, ever tried to match the hatch for this valiant gamefish?

A retired game warden friend of mine took his first Atlantic salmon, an 18-pounder, on a No. 12 dry fly, I remembered. Other fishing acquaintances swear by No. 16, 18 and even 22 wet flies for mid-summer fishing of four-and five-pound brook trout that lie in a secret, walk-in pond in our northern New England mountains. My own sport with brown trout has proven oftimes that browns prefer a 16 or 18 dry to larger sizes, when conditions dictate the use of such small patterns.

I guess somebody is going to write to me when this book is published and say: "How come? I've known about bass accepting even smaller sizes than the No. 14 Dark Hendrickson your son fished with. Why should bass be different than any other gamefish? They can be selective, like trout, and often are, my friend."

If they do, I'll reply: "Why didn't you tell me this years ago? Then I wouldn't have missed so much of this specialized kind of superb bass fishing."

Yes, experimentation often will save the day for us all.

For those commonplace, everyday bass-seeking expeditions, nevertheless, I stock my tackle boxes with an assortment of 2–0 poppers. I have read that experiments show bass can distinguish colors, so I don't feel I am being "taken" when I buy a variety of bugs in red-and-white, green (both light green and the frog imitation color), brown shades, as well as black and white, yellow, all-black, etc.

Indeed, I may even paint over poppers that I have purchased and which haven't produced as well as I think they should.

Accommodating bass poses for picture.

My bass bugs are cut so they will plop when pulled over and through the water. Some of them have tail feathers or hair tails; some have hackle around the base of the hook where it joins the cork body in front of the bended barb. Some imitate frogs; some mice; some even large moths. Others are like nothing a bass ever dreamed of, or Nature yet has conceived.

They simply appealed to me. Like all fishermen, I can get "hooked" on a lure fully as fast as any New England smallmouth or largemouth that swims.

In recent years I have become convinced of the effectiveness of fluorescent colors for all gamefish. So, I may paint a few bug bodies in blaze orange, if I don't find any available commercially readily.

As stated earlier, too, I always tote along a good assortment of big floating flies (size 4 and even 2). These may double as sea-run salmon flies but, unlike my recently acquired knowledge of using tiny trout flies for bass, I long have cast the large Wulffs successfully. The big dries can imitate many insects adequately. White Wulff for white miller moth, Gray or Brown Wulff for larger mayflies, etc. Big spent-wing patterns sometimes are attractive to bass, too, I have found.

One thing stands out in my fishing experience especially: If I find I am changing artificial lures and flies in a kind of quiet desperation, it is unlikely I will get many strikes from bass on that specific occasion. Neil's experience, when he dropped down to tiny insect imitations, is an exception in my mind to prove this point.

Surely, if conditions of weather become strikingly different (a cooling shower following several dry, hot days, for instance) then bass and other gamefish may suddenly come to life and start to hit like crazy. And, when night falls and the sun's rays are off the water, then, if ever, bass will start to feed. But, as a generalization, in an otherwise promising locale where I have consistently taken fish before, dull fishing brings on more experimentation, like: "Maybe this popper is what they want . . .", "I wonder if they will hit a big Wulff . . .", "perhaps I should change over and offer them a sinking lure"; and I realize that, doubtless as the bass are doing, I might as well have stayed in bed.

For, I do not consider either largemouth or smallmouth black bass to be as consistently selective as trout and salmon. They are voracious gamefish. Give them any reasonable offering and they'll accept it most of the time. That's why fishing for them is so satisfying: why so many different ways of fishing may be enjoyed when bass are sought. Nobody has to— wants to—keep all of the bass he brings to net or boatside, but unless there

The author fly casting for bass.

are some takers even the more ardent fishermen tire their arms of casting fruitlessly for hours on end.

So, it is essential to find out where bass are in good population; to visit such specific waters at the right times of year when possible (in New England, we emphasize, during late April, May and June and again in September: where legal, in October), and not to anticipate top-of-water action, particularly during the hot, mid-summer season.

Elsewhere in this book, as the complete reader knows, there are my suggestions and experiences on fishing deep at those times when it seems bass logically will be lying at considerable depth and in the cooler areas of lake or stream. The anecdote about my son Neil's dry fly fishing at Sand Pond in Maine occurred in a rather unusual year. Heavy and nearly continuous spring rains kept water levels much higher than normal that season. The dry weather for a few days before he arrived at the campground brought on heavy hatches of insects and for two or three days Neil and others there enjoyed fishing when bass were feeding heavily, I expect.

The day I fished with him and found the bass inactive probably indicated that it would be back to bottom-dragging lures and baits for anybody who really *must* catch bass then.

Thus, I will list a few bass waters in New England that have been productive for me and others down through the years. It is impossible for any of us to revisit every river and lake in this six-state region and to report up-to-the-minute bass fishing prospects so widely. So, I urge my readers to *check out the precise spots where fast bass fishing is currently available* by talking with fisheries' men on state levels in fish and game departments, by getting lake survey reports as they are published, by making friends with local authorities, and by employing a dependable bass-fishing guide on occasion when funds accumulate to make your fishing more fun and more productive.

Most of all, go out and actually fish for bass at every opportunity. Again, I repeat, there are no answers to the secrets of catching fish as valuable as those learned by actual experience. In this book, I can only guide you to some of the places I have fished and encourage you to try your own luck beside me, cast for cast, until we both connect, play and subdue those magnificent bronzebacks.

5

SOME NEW ENGLAND BASS WATERS

I begin to list a few of the bass fishing waters in southern New England and work north into Maine, as seasons open earlier actually if not legally, too, because the ice is out in Connecticut well before it cracks up in northern New Hampshire, Vermont and Maine.

As the State officials in Connecticut indicate, it is not only necessary to know where the bass are, but also to learn which waters may be available to the public. So, their pamphlet, "Public Access to Connecticut Fishing Waters," is a must for anglers. It is put out by the Department of Environmental Protection, Office Bldg., Hartford, CT. 06115. In the revision (Spring 1972) some of the bass waters are classified fairly and honestly as to the relative quality of fishing at that time. I am listing the better ones first and others that are *good* to *fair*. (Bass are not the only species in these lakes and ponds.)

Connecticut

Beachdale Pond, Voluntown: Excellent to good for largemouth.

Black Pond, Middlefield: Excellent for largemouth.

Candlewood Lake, New Fairfield: Excellent to good for largemouth.

Dog Pond, Goshen: Excellent for largemouth.

East Twin Lake, Salisbury: Excellent for largemouth.

Gortons Pond, East Lyme: Excellent to good for largemouth.

Hayward Lake, East Haddam: Excellent to good, for largemouth.

Lake of Isles, North Stonington: Excellent to good for largemouth.

Lake Lillinonah, Bridgewater: Exceptionally good for largemouth and smallmouth bass.

Lake Zoar, Southbury: Excellent to good for largemouth and smallmouth bass.

North Farms Reservoir, Wallingford: Excellent to good for largemouth.

Waungbumbaug Lake, Coventry: Smallmouth bass very abundant, with fish larger than three pounds common. (According to pamphlet authors referred to above, "The experienced angler should find excellent smallmouth fishing in this pond.") It should be realized that once the word gets around, gamefish in such a heavily populated state may decrease due to pressure and become more shy, harder to take.

In the foregoing classification, I have taken the liberty to alter the

Lake bass fishermen like big, able canoe.

words, "Good to excellent" to Excellent to good. "Good to fair" in the following is as published in "Public Access to Connecticut Fishing Waters," and "Good" also is unchanged. The authors of the pamphlet frequently indicate that success may depend on the experience of the sportsman. So true, anywhere!

Avery Pond, Preston: Good fishing for largemouth.

Bashan Lake, East Haddam: Good for largemouth.

Beseck Lake, Middlefield: Fair to good fishing for largemouth bass.

Bigelow Pond, Union: Fair to good for largemouth.

Billings Lake, North Stonington: Fair to poor for smallmouth bass.

Black Pond, Woodstock: Fair for smallmouth.

Crystal Lake, Ellington: Fair to poor for smallmouth and largemouth bass.
Dodge Pond, East Lyme: Fair to good for largemouth.

Dooley Pond, Middletown: Good for largemouth.

Gardner Lake, Salem-Montville: Fair to good for smallmouth.

Glasgo Pond, Griswold: Fair to good fishing for largemouth bass.

Highland Lake, Winchester: Fair for largemouth and smallmouth bass.

Holbrook Pond, Hebron: Fair for largemouth.

Lake Kenosia, Danbury: Good for largemouth.

Little Pond, Thompson: Good for largemouth.

Long Pond, North Stonington: Fair to good for largemouth bass.

Mamanasco Lake, Ridgefield: Good for largemouth.

Mashapaug Lake, Union: Fair to good for largemouth.

(It will be recalled that the state record for largemouth bass—12 lbs. 14 oz.—was caught in this pond in 1961; that a smallmouth—7 lbs. 10 oz.—was taken in 1954.

Moodus Reservoir, East Haddam: Good for largemouth.

Mudge Pond, Sharon: Fair to good for largemouth.

Naubesatuck Lake, Mansfield: Good for largemouth.

Pataganset Lake, East Lyme: Fair to good for largemouth. (Calico bass up to three pounds not uncommon. The Calico, or black crappie, is found in numerous Connecticut waters.)

Pickerel Pond, Colchester: Restocked with largemouth bass and should provide good bass fishing eventually.

Rogers Lake, Old Lyme: Good for largemouth.

Roseland Lake, Woodstock: Good for largemouth.

Squantz Pond, New Fairfield: Good for largemouth.

West Side Pond, Goshen: Good for largemouth.

Winchester Lake, Winchester: "Should" provide excellent fishing for largemouth.

Wood Creek Pond, Norfolk: Good for largemouth but weedy, numerous stumps and thus difficult to fish.

Wyassup Lake, North Stonington: Fair to good for smallmouth bass.

Rhode Island

I verified bass waters in Rhode Island with a long time friend, Tom Wright, State Fish & Wildlife section, and my choice of fishing locations met the following response from Tom:

Stafford's Pond, Tiverton: "Very good for smallmouth Bass."

Worden Pond, South Kingston (Great Swamp Management Area): "Very good: largemouth bass."

Bowdish Reservoir, George Washington Memorial State Forest (northwestern section of state): "Good for largemouth."

Flat River, Exeter: "Very good, largemouth bass."

Watchaug Pond, Burlingame State Park, Charlestown: "Both largemouth and smallmouth bass and very good fishing."

Indian Lake, near Kingston and Mooresfield in southeastern Rhode Island: "Good."

Spring Lake, Black Hut Management Area, northwestern section state, near Massachusetts line: "Fair, smallmouth."

Warwick Pond, south of Hoxie, off Alt. 117: "Good for largemouth bass."

Brickyard Pond, Barrington: "Good for largemouths."

Numerous other waters in Rhode Island have good fishing, of course. These are typical of the better possibilities.

Massachusetts

Some of the bass waters in this state—of which there actually are many —are given below, if there is either easy access or at least fair access to them.

Chequaquet Lake, Barnstable: Both largemouth and smallmouth.

Flax Pond, Bourne: Largemouth.

Garretts Pond, Barnstable: Smallmouth.

Herring Pond, Eastham: Smallmouth.

Johns Pond, Mashpee: Smallmouth.

Lawrence Pond, Sandwich: Largemouth.

Long Pond, Brewster and Harwich: Smallmouth.

Long Pond, Barnstable: Largemouth.

Long Pond, Wellfleet: Largemouth.

Long Pond, South Yarmouth: Largemouth.

Lovells Pond, Barnstable: Smallmouth.

Mystic and Middle Ponds, Barnstable: Smallmouth.

Pilgrim Lake, Provincetown: Largemouth.

Seymour Pond, Brewster: Smallmouth.

Snake Pond, Sandwich: Smallmouth.

Triangle Pond, Sandwich: Smallmouth.

Mashpee and Wakeby Ponds, Mashpee and Sandwich: Smallmouth bass.

Benedict Pond, Monterey: Largemouth.

Benton Pond, Otis: Smallmouth.

Big Pond, Otis: Smallmouth.

Lake Buel, Monterey and North Marlboro: Both kinds.

Center Pond, Becket: Smallmouth.

East Otis Reservoir, Otis and Tolland: Both kinds.

Goose Pond, Tyringham and Lee: Both kinds of bass.

Hoosac Reservoir, Lanesboro and N. Pike: Largemouth.

Laurel Lake, Lee and Lenox: Largemouth.

Lower Spectacle Pond, Sandisfield: Smallmouth.

Mansfield Pond, Great Barrington: Both kinds.

Noyes Pond, Tolland: Smallmouth.

Onota Lake, Pittsfield: Both kinds.

Pontoosuc Lake, Pittsfield: Largemouth.

Prospect Lake, Egremont: Smallmouth.

Richmond Pond, Richmond and West Pittsfield: Largemouth.

Stockbridge Bowl, Stockbridge: Both kinds.

Thousand Acre Swamp, New Marlboro: Both.

Yokum Pond, Becket: Largemouth.

Lake Nippenicket, Raynham: Largemouth.

Norton Reservoir: Largemouth.

Sabbatia Lake, Taunton: Largemouth.

Sassaquin Pond, New Bedford: Largemouth.

Warren Reservoir, Swansea: Smallmouth.

Winneconnet Pond, Norton: Both kinds.

Lake Attitash, Amesbury: Smallmouth.

Flint's Pond, Tyngsboro: Largemouth.

Forest Lake, Methuen: Smallmouth.

Foster's Pond, Andover: Largemouth.

Frye Pond, Andover: Largemouth.

Gardner Lake, Amesbury: Smallmouth.

Hood Pond, Ipswich and Topsfield: Both kinds.

Millvale Reservoir, Haverhill: Largemouth.

Pentucket Pond, Georgetown: Largemouth.

Round Pond, Haverhill: Largemouth.

Tully Pond, Orange: Largemouth.

Wickett Pond, Wendell: Largemouth.

Lake Wyola, Shutesbury: Both kinds.

Buck Pond, Westfield: Largemouth.

Chapin Pond, Ludlow: Smallmouth.

Congamond Lakes, Southwick: Largemouth.

Forest Lake, Palmer: Largemouth.

Hamilton Reservoir, Holland: Largemouth.

Hampden Ponds, Westfield: Largemouth.

Holland Pond: Both kinds.

Little Alum Pond, Brimfield: Smallmouth.

Loon Pond, Springfield: Largemouth.

Nine Mile Pond, Wilbraham: Both kinds.

Sherman Pond, Brimfield: Largemouth.

Van Horn Park Pond, Springfield: Largemouth.

Watershop Pond, Springfield: Largemouth.

Hampton Pond, Southampton and Westfield: Largemouth

Metacomet Lake, Belchertown: Largemouth.

Norwich Pond, Huntington: Smallmouth.

Plainfield Pond: Largemouth.

Quabbin Reservoir, Belchertown: Both kinds.

Upper Highland Lake, Goshen: Smallmouth.

Althea Lake, Tyngsboro: Largemouth.

Baddacook Pond, Groton: Largemouth.

Cochituate Lake, Natick: Both kinds.

Dudley Pond, Wayland: Largemouth.

Farm Pond, Framingham: Largemouth.

Fort Meadow Reservoir, Marlboro and Hudson: Largemouth.

Harbor Pond, Townsend: Largemouth.

Heard Pond, Wayland: Largemouth.

Hopkinton Reservoir, Hopkinton and Ashland: Largemouth.

Horn Pond, Woburn: Both kinds.

Knops Pond, Groton: Largemouth.

Learned Pond, Framingham: Largemouth.

Long Lake, Littleton: Largemouth.

Long Pond, Dracut and Tyngsboro: Largemouth.

Mascopic Lake, Tyngsboro and Dracut: Both kinds.

Massapoag Pond, Dunstable, Tyngsboro and Groton: Smallmouth.

Upper Mystic Lake, Winchester, Arlington and Medford: Smallmouth.

Lake Quannapowitt, Wakefield: Both kinds.

Sandy Pond, Ayer: Both kinds.

Shakum Pond, Framingham: Largemouth.

Silver Lake, Wilmington: Both kinds.

Sought-For Pond, Westford: Both kinds.

Spy Pond, Arlington: Largemouth.

Walden Pond, Concord: Smallmouth.

Whitehall Reservoir, Hopkinton: Largemouth.

Winthrop Lake, Holliston: Largemouth.

Massapoag Pond, Sharon: Largemouth.

Morse Pond, Wellesley: Largemouth.

Lake Pearl, Wrentham: Largemouth.

Pinewood Pond, Stoughton: Largemouth.

Ponkapoag Pond, Randolph and Canton: Both kinds.

Populatic Pond, Norfolk: Largemouth.

Lake Waban, Wellesley: Largemouth.

Whitman Pond, Weymouth: Largemouth.

In *Plymouth,* there are these bass waters with fair to good access: *Billington Sea,* both kinds; *Charge Pond,* smallmouth; *College Pond,* smallmouth; *Curlew Pond,* largemouth; *Dunham Pond,* largemouth; *Ezekial Pond,* largemouth; *Five Mile Pond,* largemouth; *Fresh Pond,* smallmouth; *Little Five Mile Pond,* largemouth; *West Pond,* smallmouth, and in *Plymouth and Wareham: White Island Pond,* smallmouth.

Furnace Pond, Pembroke: Both kinds.

Johns Pond, Carver, Largemouth.

Maquan Pond, Hanson: Largemouth.

Monponsett East, Halifax: Largemouth. (Also largemouth in *Monponsett West, Halifax.)*

Lake Nippenicket, Bridgewater: Largemouth.

Oldham Pond, Pembroke: Both kinds.

Sampsons Pond, Carver: Smallmouth.

Stetson Pond, Pembroke, smallmouth.

Big Alum Pond, Sturbridge: Smallmouth.

Buffumville Reservoir, Charlton: Largemouth.

Cedar Pond, Sturbridge: Largemouth.

Lake Chauncey, Westboro: Smallmouth.

Smallmouth bass are where you find them.

Demond Pond, Rutland: Largemouth.

Denison Lake, Winchendon: Both kinds.

Eagle Lake, Holden: Largemouth.

Eddy Pond, Auburn: Largemouth.

Hardwick Pond: Largemouth.

Hayden Pond, Dudley: Largemouth.

Indian Lake, Worcester: Largemouth.

Jordan Pond, Shrewsbury: Largemouth.

Kendall Pond, Gardner: Largemouth.

Lake Lashaway, East Brookfield: Both kinds.

Little Chauncy Pond, Northboro: Largemouth.

Long Pond, Rutland: Both kinds.

Long Pond, Sturbridge: Largemouth.

Nipmuc Pond, Mendon: Largemouth.

Pratt Pond, Upton: Largemouth.

Quaboag Pond, Brookfield, East: Both kinds.

Quacumquasit Lake, South Pond: Both kinds. (In *Sturbridge, Brookfield and East Brookfield.)*

Queen Lake, Phillipston: Smallmouth.

Lake Quinsigamond, Shrewsbury, Worcester and Grafton: Both kinds.

South Meadow, Mossy and Coachlace Ponds, Clinton: Both kinds.

Stiles Reservoir, Spencer: Both kinds.

Sugden Reservoir, Spencer: Smallmouth.

Thompson Pond, Spencer: Largemouth.

Walker Pond, Sturbridge: Largemouth.

Wallum Pond, Douglas: Smallmouth.
Webster Lake: Smallmouth.

West Waushacum Pond, Sterling: Largemouth.

Whitney Pond, Winchendon: Largemouth.

Winnekeag Lake, Ashburnham: Both kinds.

New Hampshire

In the more lightly populated northern New England states (New Hampshire, Vermont and Maine) access to fishing waters is not yet so serious a problem as in the preceding list. Bass fishing is good to excellent in many of the following lakes and ponds in the Granite State:

Alphabetically, then: *Armington Lake, Piermont,* smallmouth; *Ashuelot Pond, Washington,* both kinds of bass; *Ayers Pond, Barrington,* both kinds; *Baboosic Lake, Amherst,* largemouth; *Baker (Upper-Lower), Orford,* both kinds; *Bear Pond, Alton,* largemouth; *Beaver Lake, Derry,* smallmouth; *Blaisdell Lake, Sutton,* smallmouth; *Bow Lake, Strafford,* smallmouth; *Bradley Lake, Andover,* smallmouth.

Chesham Pond, Harrisville, both kinds; *Chestnut Pond, Epsom,* largemouth; *Chocorua Lake, Tamworth,* smallmouth; *Clement Pond, Hopkinton,* smallmouth; *Contoocook Lake, Jaffrey and Rindge,* largemouth; *Contoocook River, Contoocook,* smallmouth; *Conway Lake,* smallmouth; *Country Pond, Kingston,* both kinds; *Crescent Lake, Acworth and Unity,* smallmouth; *Crescent Lake, Wolfeboro,* smallmouth.

Crooked Pond, Loudon, smallmouth; *Crystal Lake, Enfield,* smallmouth; *Crystal Lake, Gilmanton,* smallmouth; *Deering Reservoir,* smallmouth; *Dudley Pond, Deering,* both kinds; *Forest Lake, Whitefield,* smallmouth; *Frost Pond, Dublin and Jaffrey,* smallmouth; *Gilman Pond, Alton,* largemouth; *Gilmore Pond, Jaffrey,* smallmouth; *Gould Pond, Hillsboro,* smallmouth; *Grafton Pond,* smallmouth; *Great East Lake, Wakefield,* smallmouth; *Gregg Lake, Antrim,* smallmouth; *Halfmoon Lake, Alton and Barnstead,* both kinds; *Harvey Lake, Northwood,* smallmouth; *Haunted Lake, Francestown,* largemouth; *Highland Lake, Stoddard,* both kinds; *Hubbard Pond, Rindge,* smallmouth; *Hunts Pond, Hancock,* smallmouth; *Indian Pond, Orford,* smallmouth; *Island Pond, Atkinson and Derry,* smallmouth; *Island Pond, Washington,* largemouth; *Jenness Lake, Northwood,* smallmouth; *Kanasatka Lake, Moultonboro,* smallmouth; *Kezar Lake, Sutton,* smallmouth; *Kingswood Lake, Brookfield,* smallmouth; *Knights Pond, Alton,* largemouth; *Kolelemook Lake, Springfield,* smallmouth; *Lily Pond, Barnstead,* largemouth; *Lily Pond, Gilford,* largemouth; *Little Bow Pond, Northwood,* largemouth; *Little Sunapee Lake, New London,* smallmouth.

Bass-fishing guide fillets catch for lunch.

Lovell Lake, Wakefield, smallmouth; *Martin Meadow Pond, Lancaster,* both kinds; *Massabesic Lake, Auburn,* smallmouth; *Massasecum Lake, Bradford,* both kinds; *May Pond, Washington,* largemouth; *Meetinghouse Pond, Marlboro,* largemouth; *Mendums Pond, Barrington,* both kinds; *Merrimack River, Boscawen, Hookset,* etc., smallmouth; *Merrymeeting Lake, New Durham,* smallmouth; *Nay Pond, Milan,* smallmouth; *North River Pond, Northwood, Barrington and Nottingham,* smallmouth; *Northwood Lake, Northwood,* both kinds; *Norway Pond, Hancock,* smallmouth; *Odiorne Pond, Epsom,* largemouth; *Onway Lake, Raymond,* smallmouth; *Ossipee Lake,* smallmouth; *Otter Lake, Greenfield,* smallmouth; *Otternick Pond, Hudson,* largemouth; *Pawtuckaway Lake, Nottingham,* both kinds; *Pearley Lake, Rindge,* largemouth; *Perkins Pond, Sunapee,* smallmouth; *Phillips Pond, Sandown,* both kinds.

Pierce Lake, Hillsboro, smallmouth; *Pleasant Lake, Deerfield,* smallmouth; *Pleasant Lake, New London,* smallmouth; *Pleasant Pond, Francestown,* smallmouth; *Pleasant Pond, Henniker,* largemouth; *Powwow River, Kingston,* largemouth; *Province Lake, Effingham,* smallmouth; *Robinson Pond, Hudson,* largemouth; *Round Pond, Wakefield,* smallmouth; *Rust Pond, Wolfeboro,* smallmouth; *Scobie Pond, Londonderry,* smallmouth; *Scott Pond, Fitzwilliam,* largemouth; *Shattuck Pond, Francestown,* largemouth; *Shingle Pond, Deerfield,* largemouth; *Silver Lake, Belmont, Northfield and Tilton,* smallmouth; *Silver Lake, Madison,* smallmouth; *Spofford Lake, Chesterfield,* both kinds.

Big and Little Squam lakes, Holderness, smallmouth; *Stevens Pond, Manchester,* both kinds; *Stinson Lake, Rumney,* smallmouth; *Sunapee Lake, Sunapee, Newbury and New London,* smallmouth; *Suncook Lakes, Barnstead,* smallmouth; *Sunrise Lake, Middleton,* largemouth; *Sunset Lake, Alton and Gilmanton,* smallmouth; *Swain's Pond, Barrington,* largemouth; *Tarleton Lake, Piermont,* smallmouth; *Taylor Pond, Hampton,* largemouth; *Thorndike Pond, Dublin and Jaffrey,* smallmouth; *Big Turkey Pond, Concord,* largemouth; *Turtletown Pond, Concord,* smallmouth; *Warren Lake, Alstead,* both kinds; *Waukewan Lake, Meredith,* smallmouth; *Weare Reservoir,* both kinds; *Webster Lake, Franklin,* smallmouth; *Wentworth Lake, Wolfeboro,* smallmouth; *Winnipesaukee Lake, Laconia,* etc., smallmouth and *Winnisquam Lake, Laconia, Sanbornton,* etc., both kinds.

Vermont

At the time this book is being written (1972) two Vermont state record bass had been recorded by the Fish and Game Department: a smallmouth from *Harriman Lake* in *Wilmington,* that weighed 6 lb. 7 oz. dressed, and a largemouth from a cove of the *Winooski River* that tipped the scales at 5 lb. 10 oz. Both were caught in 1969. These are commendable bass, particularly since they came from cool water, where fish ordinarily grow more slowly.

About the time I was writing these words, too, sportsmen "discovered" the good bass action to be had by casting in the *White River* from about *Bethel* on down to *White River Junction*, where the White flows into the Connecticut River. (Not that many bass seekers had failed to fish this section previously: just that the word only recently got around.)

For those who fly-fish, one Vermonter suggests using size 8 Marabou streamers and poppers of similar size, in the pools and back eddies of the White.

Some of the other rivers in southeastern Vermont that have good bass fishing are the *West* (comes into Connecticut near Brattleboro), *Williams River* (comes in above Bellows Falls), the *Black River* (enters the Connecticut south of Springfield).

I have referred to fishing the *Missisquoi River* in northwestern Vermont in an earlier chapter. Other rivers with fair to good bass waters in that section are the *Lamoille* (in stretches from *Morrisville to Lake Champlain)*, the *Winooski River* (where that '69 record largemouth was taken), and others.

Like the Lamoille, the Winooski flows across some two-thirds of the state and "hot" fishing spots need to be run down—both on the advice of resident sportsmen and from my own experience. Smallmouths are in the *Waterbury* section near *Bolton Dam,* for one location, as well as in the *Richmond* area and on to *Essex Junction,* near Champlain.

Smallmouth bass and frequently largemouth as well are in Vermont's Inland Sea *(Lake Champlain)* over a wide area.

As in Maine and New Hampshire, so much emphasis has been placed on trout and salmon fishing that, in many waters, bass are comparatively unexploited and thus are in good population and not shy, as they are where they are heavily fished over.

There are more than 400 lakes and ponds as well as some 8,000 miles of what honest Vermonters term "permanent" streams, up, down and across the state. Thus, a pictorial map that has each species identified with symbols can prove to be of help to anybody; especially to those who fish for bass infrequently, or in areas unfamiliar to them. This map is titled, "Vermont Guide to Fishing." The Vermont Development Dept., Montpelier 05602, should have copies available.

As in other state listings, bass are but one of several species in many of the Vermont waters. They are found (bass) as elsewhere in the shallower, warmer water sections of lakes and rivers that have multiple species.

So, on the *Connecticut River,* dividing Vermont from New Hampshire, I consider bass fishing to be more dependable from below St. Johnsbury (beginning south of where Route 5 runs beside the Connecticut) and continuing south to the Massachusetts line. Either or both smallmouth and largemouth bass in average to good numbers can be taken by careful river fishermen in this rather long stretch of water.

Unlike in Maine, which I will consider next for specific bass waters, this gamefish is found pretty much over all of Vermont, including as has been noted, even the more northerly parts of the state.

The Vermont bass fishing in streams and rivers is another plus for canoeists and, in places, for those who enjoy wading. A glance at the Guide to Fishing map referred to above will convince the sportsman of the number of lakes, ponds and rivers, as well as feeder streams and brooks, available to him. If the latter are low because of heavy runoff, usually bass will be located in the major rivers that are fed by these lesser tributaries. (This can be a consideration in sections where mountains are in the terrain.)

Use of a highway map, as a companion piece to the Guide to Fishing, is helpful, I have found.

Maine

As a generalized statement, the smallmouth is predominant over the largemouth bass in Maine. The largemouth has been stocked in only a few waters where temperatures are suitable to this kind of bass. Yet, as has been narrated in an earlier chapter, in certain places like *Belgrade Stream,* the largemouth grows to exciting weight and, in the cold waters of Maine, it is a valiant battler, nearly, if not equal to the smallmouth, I maintain.

Now, if an imaginary line is drawn west to east across a map of Maine, from below Rangeley near the New Hampshire border to below Houlton on the Maine–New Brunswick boundary, bass fishing populations may be anticipated south of such a line—yet, not in all waters, by any means. As has been repeated, stocking and management of gamefishes in New England have placed what well may be undue emphasis on what fisheries' professionals call the true "cold-water" species: brook trout, landlocked salmon, lake trout and, experimentally in rarer instances, hybrids like the splake.

This is largely because most sportsmen have wanted trout and salmon above all other gamefishes. Here are a few of the disadvantages of putting so many eggs of the same kind in a water-basket: Landlocked salmon hit surface lures following ice-out and for a few weeks afterward; then, only sporadically during the time when bass fishing may well be best. (The bass is more of an all-season fish, by far.) Salmon take on a new burst of life in the fall but, again, they are unpredictable and hard to catch on many occasions.

Eastern brook trout losses in hatcheries are costly. Wild trout waters are getting fewer every year and this fish doesn't seem to thrive when numerous cottages and other developments are built on the surrounding shore. The airplane on floats can ferry fishing parties successively to remote trout waters and pressure, pollution and overfishing result in shy trout, lower bag limits, restrictive laws, like fly-fishing only, etc. Despite these precautions trout are fewer, farther between, smaller, harder to catch and more costly every succeeding season.

Rainbows fare a little better but not always and browns in New England waters are a somewhat unsatisfactory gamefish, even if they can live in higher temperatures and despite the fact that they occasionally attain heavy weight before anglers can catch them. They are, indeed, so hard to catch that a casual fisherman hardly ever gets his limit to net and release or to take home, either.

These facts aren't meant to discredit trout and salmon—for I love to fish for them, photograph them, write about them (I authored *The Eastern Brook Trout* in 1951) but, notwithstanding my own and others' affection for the cold-water species, I know bass fight as well or better, are easier to entice to strike, are much hardier and—should I want to eat them freshly caught and filleted— they are delicious as a landlocked salmon and not too inferior in taste to trout.

So, it well may be that in the years ahead there will be more Maine waters to list for bass fishermen.

Meanwhile, there are hundreds of lakes, ponds and rivers that do contain smallmouth bass in this state, as well as a few largemouth waters.

Below the imaginary line I suggested previously, bass are in shallower places in such major lakes as *Sebago* in southwestern Maine (and, in just about every lake and pond in that section of the state); in *Androscoggin Lake,* near *Wayne;* in *Lake Auburn,* close by the city of the same name.

West Branch of St. Croix
is near New Brunswick–Maine boundary.

The so-called *Winthrop Lakes (Monmouth, Winthrop, Readfield, Mt. Vernon),* have such excellent bass waters as *Pocasset Lake, Parker Pond, Echo Lake, Torsey Pond, Lovejoy Lake, Maranacook, Annabessacook, Cobbosseecontee Lakes.*

The *Belgrades* are widely recognized for bass populations. Such waters as: *Long Pond, Great Pond, Messalonskee Lake, East and North Ponds,* are good. (Some have largemouth bass as well as smallmouth.)

North of the Belgrades, *Wesserunsett Lake* in *East Madison* is good bass fishing. The *Kennebec River,* from Madison down to Skowhegan produces bass very well.

East of the Belgrades, *Webber Pond* and *China Lake* have good bass populations. South of these lakes, numerous waters can be cited, like *Damariscotta Lake, Jefferson to Damariscotta; Pemaquid Pond, Damariscotta,* and others.

East from China Lake is *Lake St. George, Liberty.* A state park is on the lake but fishing pressure is nominal and bass are plentiful in shallower sections and along rocky shores of islands and the mainland area.

North and slightly east of Waterville, *Sebasticook Lake, Newport,* has bass fishing and the stream of the same name (East Branch flows into the Kennebec River) is good when water levels and other factors are right.

Most of the warmer water lakes and ponds east of Waterville also have bass populations.

Just north of Route 3, after crossing the *Penobscot River* at *Bucksport* is *Alamoosook Lake in Orland.* This is a good bass water, as are many of the other ponds and lakes east and north of Route 3 near Ellsworth, still further along the way. Due north of Ellsworth there are multiple waters that have bass, along with other species in some cases. *Nicatous Lake* lies in the northern part of Hancock County. One of several good bass waters in that section, it is more readily reached, perhaps, via 188, leaving Interstate 95 at West Enfield and driving east.

Now, a host of good waters that deserve attention from bass fishermen lie north and east of Nicatous Lake. In this lower eastern part of Maine (areas in Penobscot and Washington Counties to at least the southern Aroostook County line with these two) are such prominent bass lakes as:

Syslodobsis, Junior, Scraggley, West Grand, Pocumcus, Wabassus, Third Machias, Big, Pocomoonshine, Clifford, Crawford, Meddybemps, Spednic, Baskahegan, Grand Falls, Long; and the *West Branch of the St. Croix River,* to mention only a few.

Nobody would live long enough to fish all of the bass waters in Maine. In the last quarter of a century I have tried to and while I have many memorable trips, I still have more "unnamed" and (to me) still unexplored lakes, ponds and rivers to dream of visiting tomorrow . . . and tomorrow . . . and tomorrow.

So it is with all of us who live in New England and also with the thousands who come to this region for bass fishing. We must run down the "hot" spots ourselves, after accepting the advice of state officials, guides and friends among local residents.

Yet, even if we fish for bass "blindly," just trying our luck here and there in places that look "bassy" to us, we still will experience some of the better action with smallmouths in the nation. And, we will surprise ourselves, now and again, at the rather good largemouth fishing in what may appear to be the more unlikely places—not far from centers of dense population, for example.

Most of us will drop everything at the mention of good bass fishing and take off for destinations unknown. Let's continue to swap secrets, then. Okay?

6

BASS FISHING SUMMARY

New England bass fishing, like the jet age, is here to stay. In our six states it is good and, in certain instances, it may even get better as time goes on. We may learn to depend on fishing for bass increasingly, because of the manifold problems in sustaining trout and salmon fishing.

As I write this final chapter in *Bass Fishing in New England,* I find that "two of the weekly trophies awarded by the Belgrade Lakes Region, Inc. (Maine) for large fish caught by visitors went to one man on Friday (Aug. 4, 1972).

"August Branna of Cranford, N.J., won the largemouth bass trophy with a 6 lbs. 7 oz. fish, caught in Great Pond on a Rebel lure.

"Branna also won the non-bass category with a 3 lbs. 12 oz. pickerel.

"Mrs. Janice Molino of Flushing, N.Y. won the smallmouth trophy with a bass of 3 lbs. 10 oz. caught in Long Pond."

The Lakes Region Association release states further that in previous weeks in the 1972 season largemouth bass of more than five lbs. and smallmouths of three lbs. plus were taken, apparently with some consistency. Lures were such dependable ones as a hula popper and a flatfish.

Readers will remember that I have expressed my opinion that bass often lie in deeper water than many experienced anglers and authorities may believe.

Well, in substantiation of my statement, Gerry Jacques, a National Forest Service Ranger stationed in Virginia, was vacationing in Maine, his former residence, in August 1972.

According to Gene Letourneau, outdoor editor for five Maine newspapers, Jacques caught two smallmouth bass on a silver flatfish while trolling some *40 feet down*—and slowly.

Actually fishing for salmon or trout (at Great Pond in the Belgrades) Jacques was somewhat "surprised," says Gene, to find bass in such deep water, but noted that Jacques observed "there's always something new in fishing to make life attractive."

This "something new" has been explored at great length in this book. Yet, it will be recalled, I have stated, too, that there may not be anything really new—anything that somebody else hasn't tried—when it comes to catching bass in New England.

One national magazine carries a story, as I write, about catching big bass at midnight. (See my reference to fishing with Lew Colomy for Maine largemouths on that black, rainy night some years ago. The article referred to describes fast fishing for largemouth bass in Florida.)

I haven't mentioned fishing with the "Texas Rig"—use of multihooks to make sure bass will get one hook or another when they strike worms

Bob "Howdy Doody" Smith of TV fame and baseball great Ted Williams with bass from eastern Maine.

on the rig, instead of having only a single barb in their lips that might pull free. But sportsmen are using this method over a wide section of the country, I surmise. And, another nationally known writer has suggested adding a popper to the head of the worm to make it more weedless and attractive to bass.

Many people—thousands, indeed—swear by plastic worms, fished in a variety of ways.

Downeast in Maine, a nonresident sportsman fishes with ultralight spinning tackle and spoons, spinners and jointed minnows of trout size, rather than the larger ones we think of for bass.

Top-of-water worm fishing, baits below a bobber, lures commercially designed and the homemade variety dragged along the bottom of bass waters—these are but a few of the tactics bass fishermen employ at times.

Slow retrieves, especially at night, quiet plopping of poppers versus big bait-rod plugs that would awaken the dead—these and many other methods are touted by bass anglers. Each in this own experience has decided which is most rewarding, which puts most bass on his stringer, regardless of quite opposite theories others may suggest.

When largemouths are feeding in weed patches, "Uncle Josh" suggests a weedless spoon and Split-Tail Eel, as effective. He maintains that bass will be in such spots even in hot weather.

(A friend of ours took a four-pound smallmouth in western Maine one July evening, while fishing a popper against a patch of weeds only a few feet deep.)

If frogs are noisy in a dependable bass lake, it can be an indication that largemouths especially will be nearby, and a live frog or porkrind imitation can be a killer then.

I believe that, normally, bass will take any of the natural baits found in the waters they inhabit. This seems odd, because in certain places the supply of food for bass is so abundant it could be assumed they would be gorged on crawfish, minnows, frogs, or whatever, and have little enthusiasm for more of the same. Nevertheless, as we all know, a bait hooked on a barb and trolled, cast, jigged or floated, does have strong appeal for both largemouths and smallmouths, in spite of the largesse provided by Nature.

Uncertainty and experimentation give bass fishing much of its challenge and excitement. So often, the unusual bait, fly or popper produces for us and soon it becomes one of our "usual" offerings.

Readers will remember my anecdote about "Artie" MacKenzie and his habit of changing lures almost constantly. He caught lots of fish, too.

But in my opinion, it is especially important to give proven baits, artificial lures, and flies a good try before beginning to experiment with everything under the sun. Artie MacKenzie's success in catching fish was due in large part, I believe, to his knowledge of the specific locations and depths of water in which bass would be found on any given occasion. When they failed to strike, knowing they were "there," he changed lures until he found something they would take. Not many of us have such intimate understanding of where bass "live" at all times of year. So, we keep fishing with dependable offerings and, once we have caught bass, we try to remember the spot next time we visit the same piece of water.

To sum up this book, I emphasize: *Go fishing for bass at every opportunity.* Practice makes perfect, as it does in every pastime.

And, I have emphasized that a day is better than a few hours; that the night may well come on and find us still fishing, if we are to be successful on any given occasion.

Once, fishing for striped bass in a New Hampshire tidal river, a friend and I began trolling at noon. We didn't take a striper until 12:30 that night. Then they began hitting so fast we couldn't keep up with the action. If we had wanted to be selfish, we could have filled our boat with the stripers. All this after going fish-less for 12½ hours.

There are, then, peak feeding times for fresh-water bass, as with any other gamefish. It is possible to catch reluctant smallmouths and large-mouths that are sated with food, but it takes a lot more teasing than it does when they are hungry and just beginning to swallow everything in their sight.

What tackle can be used most effectively? I have said that this is a matter of individual preference. Indeed, to be most successful, it doubtless is better to fish for bass with equipment that you are most adept at using. If you have done only bait-casting, you probably should fish with a bait rod most of the time; gradually, if you want, switch and devote a few hours a day to spin-casting, spinning or fly fishing.

It is good to be reasonably efficient with any and all tackle, of course.

My personal preference is flyrod fishing. Now, this is not only because I have used such tackle most but that I find this sport sharper, the bass better fighters on flies and little poppers than on other rods and artificials. (Light spinning tackle provides similar sport, of course.)

Yet, like you, if nothing else will save a day for me, I will use a variety of baits—fished all the way from surface to the bottom. (Long since, I must confess, I have "graduated" from bait fishing for trout and salmon. Bass are other gamefishes entirely and demand different approaches.)

In many New England waters both or either of smallmouths and largemouths may be caught. Readers will be familiar with others, I expect, and will "discover" more lakes, ponds and streams than I could possibly list.

Should you wish to obtain travel and fishing information from official sources, besides those mentioned, you might visit Chamber of Commerce offices in the regions you plan to fish. Or, write to them.

Then, at state level, here are the contacts for such generalized information and booklets, maps, etc.:

Maine Publicity Bureau, Portland; New Hampshire Division of Economic Development, Concord 03301; Vermont Development Dept., Montpelier 05602; Massachusetts Dept. of Commerce, Boston 02202; Rhode Island Development Council, Tourist Division, Roger Williams Bldg., 49 Hayes St., Providence 02908; Connecticut Development Commission, Hartford 06115.

GOOD FISHING!

And now to Frank's last cast . . .

Some sportsmen enjoy freshly caught bass for cookout lunch; return most others to New England waters.

LAST CAST! *by Frank Woolner*

Bob Elliot has wrapped it up, and this short section is simply a caboose coupled to a lovely train of chapters. If you choose, it is a foreword in reverse—or maybe an afterword. Has anyone ever done that? We scorn arbitrary fashion in New England: we set our own fashions!

What about black bass in our northeastern states? Are they phasing out, victims of "progress" and pollution? Will our children's children find them in well remembered waters? Have those of us who are grey at the temples (Bob and I qualify) really seen the best fishing for bronzebacks?

Certainly we've enjoyed grand sport, and we'll see more before that first cast into the River Styx. *I wonder whether they'll be largemouths or smallmouths?*

Old boys sometimes sound a warning, but I don't think we'll do that. I haven't discussed the matter with Bob, because he's traveling somewhere out in the deep blue—working harder than a stripling of thirty, but I don't need a conference to guess his conclusions. Elliot thinks positively and he never adopts a parrot line.

Sure, we're going to lose waters to pollution and the questionable thing called progress. There will be more fishermen, and therefore more pressure on a renewable resource. There'll be hot spots that endure for a few years and then simmer down into obscurity. What's really new?

Something of importance! Like the ruffed grouse, another native of New England, the bronzeback is pretty self-sufficient: he can get along without state or federal fish hatcheries, and he thrives wherever the habitat is reasonably favorable. He is tolerant of temperature variations and—particularly in the largemouth—can survive a measure of pollution that would kill the more delicate trout.

Black bass adapt: they swarm happily in all sorts of ponds, lakes and brawling streams. The smallmouth prefers clean, cold water, and the largemouth will prosper in marginal puddles where mankind's depredations are obvious. Both species are plentiful, and both will remain abundant long after certain other fresh-water gamefishes have finned down that long and sorry road to extinction.

A black bass is intelligent, and that makes all of the difference. Researchers have found that a bronzeback quickly learns which artificial baits are deadly—and scorns them. This is the reason why a lure that is Murder-Incorporated for a few seasons suddenly becomes just another hunk of ordnance.

We deal with a resident gamefish. Often ponds thought to be fished out by the great majority of anglers will yield fine catches to advanced practitioners. Bob's favored streamer fly and popping bug remain effective because—and he may hate me for saying so—a very few sportsmen use them! For every man who casts a fly or a floating bug, there are one hundred who throw lures or use natural baits.

All enjoy royal sport with black bass, and those of us who write about angling extol every method. There is just as much skill employed in presenting a live hellgrammite on a small, live-lined hook as in dropping a buoyant bug into a spawning bed from sixty feet. The plug-caster who drops his lure into a hat-sized opening at maximum range is no more a miracle worker than the guy who steers a carefully hooked redfin shiner into a drop-off location where the grand bronzebacks are feeding. Regardless of tackle and lure, a fisherman can be a duffer or a champion. Little luck is involved: successful anglers are craftsmen who have learned a trade.

Black bass are handicapped by the very fact that they are plentiful! One always seeks fish that are hard to get or exotic. No trout can match the smashing surface strike of a largemouth, and no trout ever jumps as furiously as a smallmouth. If the bass happened to be rare—then it would be one of the most exclusive of the exotics!

Thank Heaven *Micropterus* is far from rare. Anglers take black bass across the length and the breadth of America, during every month of the year. Where New England states permit ice fishing, bronzeback are taken on tip-ups and jigging sticks—disciplines that introduce a whole new set of tactics and techniques. Obviously, winter bass seem to feed most ardently during any period of abnormal thaw. Evidently snowmelt, flooding into great ponds and trigger an appetite dimly remembered from the feast days of high summer.

Expect to find largemouth bass in fairly deep water during early spring, and again in the fall when temperatures are low. They repair to shallow spawning beds about lilac time and will then remain on shoal grounds through much of the summer. Every largemouth is a prowler of pad-beds and weedy jungle growth, leaving cover only during the night hours to drift through thin open water searching for hapless minnows, frogs, swimming mice, night moths and a wide assortment of other forage.

Smallmouths also provide spectacular action while guarding their nests in the spring—a reflex action probably triggered by anger rather than hunger. Unlike the largemouth, these acrobats of the tribe usually repair to deeper water immediately after spawning is completed. They can still be taken on surface lures, usually well out in some open lake over a rocky reef in bright sunlight, or during the dark-time hours when all bass like to cruise shorelines in search of food.

Black bass fishing can be spectacular in New England, yet smart anglers always search for a "hot" pond. The great ones usually do not remain great for very long, and nobody knows why. Often the transition is predictable. First, bass fishing is superb and heavyweights plentiful. Then, after a short passage of years, enthusiasts discover that bronzebacks are still abundant, but that individual sizes have decreased. There is a point at which the sportsman seeks a new stamping ground, declaring that the old bonanza is now loaded with minnows.

Fortunately, there is a flip-side to this record—for a surprising number of supposedly fished-out ponds suddenly begin to produce trophies again. For a short while this knowledge will be guarded by a handful of experts: then word gets out and the whole process is repeated.

There are trends in angling, as in all other sports. Bronzebacks enjoyed a popularity peak in southern New England during the '20s and '30s. At the same time there was a studious lack of interest in Maine, New Hampshire and Vermont—a northern area whose anglers were then mesmerized by trout and salmon.

Now the situation is reversed! There is a tremendous upsurge of interest in northern smallmouths and a general simmering down of zeal for the more southerly largemouth. Of course specialists in both regions continue to hunt a magnificent gamefish, and they know that the fickle multitudes will be back.

Possibly light angler pressure in the southern New England states at this writing may be traced to a burgeoning interest in marine sport, particularly a quest for striped bass. Some thousands of residents in Massachusetts, Rhode Island and Connecticut, many of whom cut their angling teeth on black bass with plug-casting tackle, went to the striper immediately after World War II—and have never returned to sweet water. They're missing something very good, and many are now renewing acquaintances with the old ogre of the pad-beds and the rocky reefs.

Black bass will be with us in New England, as the Indians said, so long as grass grows and water flows. They will be with us because they are tough, resilient, adaptable warriors. They are plentiful now, and they will remain abundant throughout this six-state region during the foreseeable future.

It is pretty certain that there will be a greater utilization of fly-casting tackle as the years march on, simply because this gear provides wonderful sport. For practical, as well as sporting reasons, dedicated fishermen will also keep the plug-casting outfit well up front as a weapons system. Although millions of enthusiasts will catch bass on spinning gear, there will be a steady phase-out of this rig because it is inferior to other techniques in the delivering of flies, popping bugs, spoons, rubber worms and plugs on great black bass grounds.

As Americans (and New England Yankees) we are going to recognize the black bass as the excellent game fish it is. We do so now! But there are thousands who place trout and salmon on a pedestal, forgetting that these patrician battlers are often stocked to the rod and are far from spawn of the wild.

Bass are stocked too, but never in the number of salmonids. Most of those we catch are creatures of a clean, aboriginal water-wilderness. They are cold, hard, jut-jawed brawlers with no fins clipped by hatchery workmen. If any fish can be called smart, extend that compliment to the bronzeback. They'll be around! Like the self-sufficient ruffed grouse and woodcock, bass are likely to survive adversity and "progress."

A sportsman treasures many moments afield: the game bird towering in a flame of autumn foliage; an Atlantic salmon coming clear like a curved bar of silver; black ducks setting their wings and dropping into the blocks. All are incredibly etched on a man's memory.

Is anything really better than a tremendous largemouth bass bombing the surface into a cauldron of white foam as he grabs a plug in the puckerbrush? Or a smallmouth on a popping bug, all slim, living-green fury and high, spattering jumps?

Obviously, I love bass, and I think you will agree that Bob Elliot has produced a lovely book about a lovely fish. If this truly and literally had to be a last cast, I'm not so very sure that I would not aim it at a bronzeback!